Concerning Sin, Righteousness, and Judgment

*"And He, when He comes,
will convict the world concerning
sin and righteousness and
judgment..."*

(John 16:8)

Holiness and Power Series (Introduction 1)

Concerning Sin, Righteousness, and Judgment

The Two Week Special Revival Sermon Series - 1

Dr. Jaerock Lee

Concerning Sin, Righteousness, and Judgment by Dr. Jaerock Lee
Published by Urim Books (Representative: Kyungtae Noh)
73, Yeouidaebang-ro 22-gil, Dongjak-gu, Seoul, Korea
www.urimbooks.com

All rights reserved. This book or parts thereof may not be reproduced in any form, stored in a retrieval system, or transmitted in any form or by any means, electronic, mechanical, photocopying, recording or otherwise, without prior written permission of the publisher.

Unless otherwise noted, all Scripture quotations are taken from the Holy Bible, NEW AMERICAN STANDARD BIBLE, ®, Copyright © 1960, 1962, 1963, 1968, 1971, 1972, 1973, 1975, 1977, 1995 by The Lockman Foundation. Used by permission.

Copyright © 2016 by Dr. Jaerock Lee
ISBN: 979-11-263-0186-7 04230
ISBN: 979-11-263-0185-0 (set)
Translation Copyright © 2013 by Dr. Esther K. Chung. Used by permission.

First Published in December 2016

Previously published in Korean in 2009 by Urim Books in Seoul, Korea

Edited by Dr. Geumsun Vin
Designed by Design Team of Urim Books
For more information contact: urimbook@hotmail.com

Author's Note

Praying that the readers will become righteous persons who receive God's great love and blessings...

When the great reformist, Martin Luther was young, he experienced a traumatic event. One day, while he and his friend stood under a tree to avoid the rain, lightning struck, and his friend, who was next to him, died. Due to this event, Luther became a monk, and he suffered from fear of the God who judges and condemns sin. Even though he spent a great deal of time in the confessional, he could not find a solution to the problem of sin. No matter how much he studied the Bible, he could not find an answer to the question, "How can an unrighteous man please the righteous God?"

Then one day, while reading one of Paul's letters, he finally found the peace he was looking for so hard. It is stated in Romans 1:17, *"For in it the righteousness of God is revealed from faith to faith; as it is written, 'But the righteous man shall live by faith.'"* Luther became enlightened about "God's righteousness". Although up to this point he had only known about the righteousness of God that judges all people, he now realized the righteousness of God that freely gives forgiveness of sin to all people who believe in Jesus Christ, and He even calls them 'righteous'. After this realization, Luther lived with an undying passion for the truth.

In this way, not only does God freely acknowledge those who believe in Jesus Christ as 'righteous'; but He also gives them the Holy Spirit as a gift so they may know about sin, righteousness, and judgment, so that they can voluntarily obey God and fulfill His will. Therefore we should not stop at just receiving Jesus Christ and being *called* righteous. It is very important to become a truly righteous person by casting out the sin and evil from within us with the help of the Holy Spirit.

For the last 12 years God has had our church hold a two-week special revival every year so that all the church members could receive the blessing of becoming righteous people through faith. He led us to the point where we could receive answers to all kinds of prayers we lifted up to Him. He also led us to understand the different dimensions of the spirit, goodness, light, and love, so that we could receive God's power in our lives. And, with each passing year as we made our strides of faith toward holiness and power, God blessed many people of all nations to experience the power of God that is recorded in the Bible and transcends time and space.

We published the revival sermon series, "Holiness and Power", which contains the message of God's deep providence, so the readers can systematically learn about them. The revival messages from the first three years serve as an "Introduction." They are concerned with going toward the way of true righteousness by abolishing the wall of sin between us and God. Then, the messages from the next four years teach about working toward holiness and power, which serves as the "Core Message". Lastly, the messages from the last five years will cover how to experience God's power by practicing the Word. It will serve as the "Application" part of this publication.

Today, there are many people who go on with their lives not even knowing what sin is, what righteousness is, and what judgment is all about. Even those who go to church don't have assurance of salvation, and they live secular lives—just like everyone else in the world. Furthermore, they do not lead Christian lives that are righteous according to God, but righteous according to what they think is righteous. So

Concerning Sin, Righteousness, and Judgment is the first book of the Holiness and Power sermon series which deals with how we can lead a successful Christian life by receiving forgiveness for our sins and by accomplishing the righteousness of God in our lives.

To confirm this teaching with evidence of His power, in the first session of the first day of our revival in 1993, God promised the blessing of conception for dozens of couples who were married for 5-6 years, and even as long as 10 years without conceiving a child. By the end of the revival, almost all of these couples conceived and began raising families.

I'd like to thank Geumsun Vin, the Director of the Editorial Bureau and her staff for their hard work in making the publication of this book possible, and I pray in the name of the Lord that many people who read this book can solve their problem of sin, thereby receiving answers to all of their prayers!

March 2009

Jaerock Lee

Introduction

This book, titled *Concerning Sin, Righteousness, and Judgment*, consists of five chapters dedicated to each topic of sin, righteousness, and judgment. This book explains in detail how one can find the solution to the problem of sin, how one can live a life of blessing by becoming a righteous person, and how one can avoid the coming judgment and enjoy eternal blessings instead.

The first chapter concerning sin is titled "Salvation". It explains why man needs to be saved and the true meaning and method of receiving salvation. The chapter that immediately follows, "The Father, Son, and Holy Spirit", guides the reader to correctly understand how God's power and authority, the name of Jesus Christ, and the guidance of the Holy Spirit all work together as the Triune God, so one can receive a clear solution to the problem of sin and walk the correct way toward salvation.

The chapter titled "Works of the Flesh" analyzes and explains the subject of wall of sin that stands between man and God. The next chapter, titled "Therefore Bear Fruit in Keeping with Repentance", explains the importance of bearing fruit in keeping with repentance in order to reach complete salvation through Jesus Christ.

The last chapter concerning sin, titled, "Abhor What is Evil; Cling to What is Good", teaches the reader to cast off evil which is displeasing to God, and to act with goodness, according to the Word of truth.

Next, in the first chapter dealing with righteousness, "Righteousness That Leads to Life", makes clear how we—all mankind—receive eternal life through the righteous act of Jesus Christ. In the chapter titled, "The Righteous Shall Live By Faith", it explains the importance of realizing that salvation can only be received through faith; and thus the reason we must obtain true faith.

Chapter 8, "To the Obedience of Christ", explains one must break down fleshly thoughts and theories and just obey the Christ so that he can have true faith and enjoy a prosperous life full of blessings and answers to prayers. Chapter 9, "He Whom the Lord Commends", takes a closer look at the lives of several patriarchs of faith, while teaching the reader how one must act in order to become a person commended by God. The last chapter, concerning righteousness, is titled "Blessing". It is an observation of the life and faith of Abraham—the father of faith and the seed of blessings—followed by some practical ways in which a believer can come to enjoy a life of blessings.

In the first chapter concerning judgment, titled "The Sin of Disobeying God", delves into the consequences that follow when man commits the sin of going against God. The next chapter, "I Will Blot out Man from the Face of the Land", describes God's judgment which follows when the wickedness of man reaches its limit.

The chapter titled "Do Not Go against His Will", tells the readers that God's judgment comes when one goes against the will of God; that they should realize what a great blessing it is to obey God's will and can become obedient to God. In the chapter titled "Thus Says the LORD of Hosts", the author explains in detail how one can receive healing and answers to prayers. He also explains the importance of becoming a righteous person who fears God.

And the last chapter, *"Concerning Sin, Righteousness, and Judgment",* unlocks the way to solve the problem of sin; becoming a righteous person; meeting the living God; the way to avoid the Final Judgment to come; and receiving a life of eternal blessings.

This book explains specific ways in which we who have accepted Jesus Christ and received the Holy Spirit can receive salvation and eternal life, answers to prayers, and blessings. I pray in the name of the Lord that through this book, many people will become righteous men and women who are pleasing to God!

March, 2009
Geumsun Vin,
Director of Editorial Bureau

Author's Note
Introduction

Part 1 Concerning Sin...

Chapter 1 Salvation · 3

The Creator God and man
The wall of sin between God and man
The true meaning of salvation
The method of salvation
The providence of salvation through Jesus Christ

Chapter 2 The Father, Son, and Holy Spirit · 13

Who is the Father God?
Father God - the supreme director of human cultivation
Who is the Son, Jesus Christ?
Jesus Christ the Savior
Who is the Holy Spirit, the Helper?
The Work of the Holy Spirit, the Helper
God the Trinity fulfills the providence of salvation

Chapter 3 Works of the Flesh · 27

Things of the flesh and works of the flesh
Works of the flesh that keep man from inheriting the kingdom of God
Evident works of the flesh

Chapter 4 "Therefore Bear Fruit in Keeping with Repentance" · 47

Bear fruit in keeping with repentance
Do not suppose Abraham is your father
"Every tree that does not bear good fruit is cut down and thrown into the fire"
The fruit in keeping with repentance
People who bore the fruits in keeping with repentance

Chapter 5 "Abhor What is Evil; Cling to What is Good." · 63

How evil is displayed as sin
To cast out evil and become a person of goodness
An evil and adulterous generation that craves a sign
The forms of evil we should abhor

Glossary 1

Part 2 Concerning Righteousness...

Chapter 6 Righteousness That Leads to Life · 83

Righteousness in God's sight
The one act of righteousness which saves all of mankind
The beginning of righteousness is believing in God
The righteousness of Jesus Christ which we must emulate
The way of becoming a righteous person
The blessings for the righteous

Chapter 7 The Righteous Shall Live By Faith · 97

To become a truly righteous person
Why do we need to become righteous?
The righteous shall live by faith
How to possess spiritual faith
Ways to live by faith

Chapter 8 To the Obedience of Christ · 109

Fleshly thoughts which are hostile toward God
"Self-Righteousness" – one of the prime fleshly thoughts
Apostle Paul broke down his fleshly thoughts
The righteousness which comes from God
Saul disobeyed God with fleshly thoughts
The way to fulfill God's righteousness through faith

Chapter 9 He Whom the Lord Commends · 123

He whom the Lord commends
To be approved by God
Nail your passions and desires on the cross
The patriarchs who were righteous before God

Chapter 10 Blessing · 137

Abraham, the Father of Faith
God considers faith as righteousness and gives His blessings
God makes quality vessels through trials
God prepares a way out, even during trials
God blesses even during trials
Abraham's character of vessel

Glossary 2, 3

Part 3 Concerning Judgment...

Chapter 11 The Sin of Disobeying God · 155

Adam, the man created in God's image
Adam ate the forbidden fruit
The result of Adam's sin of disobeying God
The reason God put the tree of the knowledge of good and evil
The way to be free from the curse caused by sin
The result of Saul's sin of disobedience toward God
The result of Cain's sin of disobedience towards God

Chapter 12 "I Will Blot Out Man from the Face of the Land" · 167

The difference between an evil person and a good person
Why God's judgment comes
* Because the wickedness of man was great
* Because the thought of the heart is evil
* Because every intent of the heart is always evil
To avoid God's judgment

Chapter 13 Do Not Go Against His Will · 179

Judgment comes when we stand against God's will
People who went against God's will

Chapter 14 "Thus Says the LORD of Hosts..." · 193

God rejects the proud
King Hezekiah's pride
The pride of believers
The pride of false prophets
The judgment for people who act with pride and evil
The blessings of the righteous who fear God

Chapter 15 Concerning Sin, Righteousness, and Judgment · 203

Concerning sin
Why He judges concerning sin
Concerning righteousness
Why He judges concerning righteousness
Concerning judgment
The Holy Spirit convicts the world
Cast out sin and live a life of righteousness

Glossary 4

Part 1
Concerning Sin...

"... concerning sin, because they do not believe in Me;"
(John 16:9)

"If you do well, will not your countenance be lifted up? And if you do not do well, sin is crouching at the door; and its desire is for you, but you must master it." (Genesis 4:7)

"'Only acknowledge your iniquity, that you have transgressed against the LORD your God and have scattered your favors to the strangers under every green tree, and you have not obeyed My voice,' declares the LORD." (Jeremiah 3:13)

"Truly I say to you, all sins shall be forgiven the sons of men, and whatever blasphemies they utter; but whoever blasphemes against the Holy Spirit never has forgiveness, but is guilty of an eternal sin." (Mark 3:28-29)

"'But, so that you may know that the Son of Man has authority on earth to forgive sins,' He said to the paralytic 'I say to you, get up, and pick up your stretcher and go home.'" (Luke 5:24)

"Afterward Jesus found him in the temple and said to him, 'Behold, you have become well; do not sin anymore, so that nothing worse happens to you.'" (John 5:14)

"Do you not know that when you present yourselves to someone as slaves for obedience, you are slaves of the one whom you obey, either of sin resulting in death, or of obedience resulting in righteousness?" (Romans 6:16)

"My little children, I am writing these things to you so that you may not sin. And if anyone sins, we have an Advocate with the Father, Jesus Christ the righteous; and He Himself is the propitiation for our sins; and not for ours only, but also for those of the whole world." (1 John 2:1-2)

Chapter 1

Salvation

> *"And there is salvation in no one else; for there is no other name under heaven that has been given among men by which we must be saved."*
> (Acts 4:12)

In this world, depending on the religion and culture, people worship all kinds of different idols; there is even an idol called 'the god we don't know' (Acts 17:23). Today, a religion called the 'The Emerging Religion', a religion created from the mixture of doctrines of many religions, is drawing much attention, and many people have accepted 'religious pluralism', which is based on the philosophy that there is salvation in all religions. However, the Bible tells us that the Creator God is the one true God, and that Jesus Christ is the one and only Savior (Deuteronomy 4:39; John 14:6; Acts 4:12).

The Creator God and man

God definitely exists. Just as we exist because our parents gave birth to us, mankind exists in this world because God created us.

When we look at a small watch, we see that the tiny parts in the watch intricately work together to tell the time. But no one will look at the watch and think that it just accidentally came together by itself. Even a small watch can exist in this world because someone designed it and made it. Then what about the universe? Incomparable to the small watch, the universe is so complex and so vast that the human mind cannot imagine all of its mysteries or even grasp its scale. The fact that the solar system, which is just one small part of the universe, operates so precisely without a fraction of a mistake, makes it very hard not to believe in God's creation.

The human body is the same. All the organs, cells, and many other elements are arranged so perfectly and work together so intricately that their arrangement and functions are a true wonder. Yet, with all the things that man has discovered about the human body is only a fraction of all there is to uncover. So how can we say something like the human anatomy just randomly came to be?

Let me share a simple illustration that everyone can easily acknowledge. On a person's face, there are two eyes, one nose, two nostrils, one mouth, and two ears. Their arrangement is such that the eyes are on the very top, the nose is in the center, the mouth is under the nose, and the ears are placed one on each side of the face. This is the same, whether we are Black, Caucasian, or Asian. This is not only true for people. This is the same for animals like lions, tigers, elephants, dogs, etc., and for birds like eagles and doves, and even for fish.

If Darwinian evolution were true, animals, birds, and human beings must have evolved differently each in their own way according to their environments. But why are the appearance and arrangement of the faces so much alike? This is the overpowering evidence that the one and only Creator God designed and created all of us. The fact that we were all created in the same image shows us that the Creator is not several beings, but one being.

Originally I was an atheist. I heard people say that if you go to church you can receive salvation. However, I did not even know what salvation was, or how to receive it. Then one day, my stomach became dysfunctional from overdrinking, and eventually I had to spend the next seven years bedridden, and sick. Every night, my mother poured water into a bowl, looked toward the Big Dipper, and rubbing her hands together, she prayed and prayed for my healing. She even gave large sums of money to the Buddhist temple, but my sickness just got worse and worse. I was not saved from this desperate situation by the Big Dipper nor was I saved by Buddha. It was God. The moment my mother heard that I was healed after going to church, she threw away all of her idols and went to church. This was because she realized that only God was the one true God.

The wall of sin between God and man

Despite the fact that there is such clear evidence that the Creator God, who created the heavens and the earth, exists, why is it that people won't believe in Him or meet Him? This is because there is a wall of sin blocking the relationship between God and man. Because the Creator God is righteous, and He has absolutely no sin, if we have sin, we cannot communicate with Him.

Occasionally there are people who think, "I have no sin." Just as we cannot see a stain on our shirt if we are standing in a dark room, if we are standing in the midst of the darkness that is untruth, we cannot see our sins. So if we say we believe in God and yet our spiritual eyes are still closed, then we cannot discover our sins. We are just going to and from church, meaninglessly. The result? We attend church for 10, or even 20 years without meeting God and without receiving answers to any of our prayers.

The God of love wants to meet us, talk to us, and answer our prayers. This is why God is earnestly asking each of us, "Please break down the wall of sin between you and Me so we can freely share conversations of love. Please make a way for Me to take away the pain and suffering you are embracing right now."

Let's say that a little child is trying to put a piece of thread through the eye of a needle. This is a hard task for a young child. But, it is a relatively easy task for the child's parent. But no matter how much the parent wants to help the child, if a huge wall is standing between the two of them, the parent cannot help his child. Likewise, if a huge wall of sin is standing between us and God, we cannot receive any answers to our prayers. So first and foremost, we must solve this sin problem, and then we must receive the ultimate solution to the most important issue of salvation.

The true meaning of salvation

In our society, the word 'salvation' is used in many different ways. When we save a drowning person or help someone recover from a business failure or help someone in a family crisis, we sometimes say that we 'saved' them.

Then what does the Bible call being 'saved'? According to the Bible, it is lifting mankind from sin. Namely, it is bringing them within borders of the place where God wants them to be, where they can receive the solution to the problem of sin and enjoy eternal joy in Heaven. So to put it in simple spiritual terms, the entrance to salvation is Jesus Christ, and the house of salvation is Heaven, or God's kingdom.

In John 14:6, Jesus said, *"I am the way, and the truth, and the life; no one comes to the Father but through Me."* Therefore salvation is to go to Heaven through Jesus Christ.

Many people evangelize and emphasize the importance of receiving salvation. So why do we need salvation? It is because our spirits are immortal. When people die, their soul and spirit separate from their body, and those who received salvation go to Heaven, and those who didn't receive salvation go to Hell. Heaven is God's kingdom where there is eternal joy, and Hell is a place of eternal pain and suffering, consisting of the lake of fire and brimstone (Revelations 21:8).

Because Heaven and Hell are places that actually exist, there are people who have seen Heaven and Hell through visions, and there are many people whose spirits actually visited those places. If someone thinks that all these people are lying, they are simply being stubborn. Since the Bible clearly explains about both Heaven and Hell, we need to believe. The Bible, unlike any other book, contains the message of salvation—the words of the Creator God.

The Bible records the creation of mankind, and how God has worked thus far. It clearly explains the complete process of how man had sinned, corrupted and become subject to eternal death, and how God saved him. It records the events of the past, the present, the future, and God's ultimate judgment in the end times.

Yes, it is important that we live peacefully without any problems in this world. However, compared to Heaven, the life we live in this world is very short, and temporary. Ten years seems like a long time, but when we look back, it seems like just yesterday. The rest of our time here on earth is the same. Though a person may live and work hard and gain many things, they will all perish when the lifetime here on earth is finished. So, what good are they?

No matter how much we possess and gain, we cannot take it with us to the eternal world. And even if we gain fame and power, when we die, all of that will eventually fade away and become forgotten.

The method of salvation

Acts 4:12, *"And there is salvation in no one else; for there is no other name under heaven that has been given among men by which we must be saved."* The Bible tells us that Jesus Christ is the only Savior who can save us. Then why is salvation only possible in the name of Jesus Christ? This is because the problem of sin must be solved. In order to better understand this, let us go back to the time of Adam and Eve, the root of mankind.

After creating Adam and Eve, God gave Adam the power and glory to rule over all the created things. And for a long time, they lived in the abundance of the Garden of Eden until one day they fell into the serpent's scheme and ate the fruit of the knowledge of good and evil. After disobeying God by eating the fruit that God forbade them to eat, sin entered into them (Genesis 3:1-6).

Romans 5:12 states, *"Just as through one man sin entered into the world, and death through sin, and so death spread to all men, because all sinned."* Because of Adam, sin came into this world and all of mankind came to sin. So as a result, death came to all mankind.

God did not simply save these people from sin without any conditions. Romans 5:18-19 says, *"So then as through one transgression there resulted condemnation to all men, even so through one act of righteousness there resulted justification of life to all men. For as through the one man's disobedience the many were made sinners, even so through the obedience of the One the many will be made righteous."*

This means that just as all of mankind became sinners because of the sin of one man, Adam, through the obedience of one man, all of mankind can be saved as well. God is the head of all created things, but He makes all things happen in a proper order (1 Corinthians 14:40); therefore He prepared one man who had all the qualifications of being the Savior—and that was Jesus Christ.

The providence of salvation through Jesus Christ

Among the spiritual laws, there is a law that says, *"the wages of sin is death"* (Romans 6:23). On the flipside, there is also a law for redeeming one from this sin. What is directly related to this spiritual law is the law on the redemption of the land in Israel. This law allows a person to sell land, but not permanently. If a person sold his land because of economic hardships, at any time, another one of his rich relatives can always buy it back for him. And if he has no rich relatives that can do this for him, he can always buy it back if and when he regains his wealth (Leviticus 25:23-25).

Redemption from sin works the same way. If anyone is qualified to redeem his brother from sin, he can. But whoever it is, that someone must pay for the price of the sin.

But as it is written in 1 Corinthians 15:21, *"For since by a man came death, by a man also came the resurrection of the dead,"* the one who could save us from sin has to be a man. This is why Jesus came into this world in the flesh—in the form of a man who became a sinner.

A person who has debt himself does not have the ability to pay off the debt for someone else. Likewise, a person with sin cannot redeem mankind from sin. A person not only inherits the physical features and personality traits of his parents, but also their sinful natures as well. If we observe a small child and we see another child sit on that child's mother's lap, the child becomes uneasy and tries to push the other child off his mother's lap. Even though no one taught him to do that, jealousy and envy naturally comes out of him. Some babies, when they become hungry and they are not fed right away, they begin to cry uncontrollably. This is because of the sinful nature of rage that they inherited from their parents. These types of sinful natures people inherit from their parents through their life-force are called 'original sin'. All descendants of Adam are born with this original sin; therefore none of them can redeem another from sin.

However, Jesus was born through conception by the Holy Spirit, so He did not inherit this original sin from any parent. And, while He was growing up, He obeyed all the laws; therefore He did not commit any type of sin. In the spiritual realm, having no sin in this way is power.

Jesus received the punishment of crucifixion with joy because He had the kind of love that did not spare even His own life to redeem the mankind from sin. In order to redeem man from the curse of the Law, He died on the wooden cross (Galatians 3:13) and shed His precious blood that was untainted from original sin or self-committed sins. He paid for all of the sins of all mankind.

In order to save the sinners, God did not even spare the life of His one and only Son by death upon the cross. This is the great love He bestowed upon us. And Jesus proved His love for us by giving up His own life in order to become the peace offering between us and God. Besides Jesus, there is no one else who has this kind of love, or the power to redeem us from sin. These are the reasons why it is only through Jesus Christ that we can receive salvation.

Chapter 2

The Father, Son, and Holy Spirit

"But the Helper, the Holy Spirit, whom the Father will send in My name, He will teach you all things, and bring to your remembrance all that I said to you."
(John 14:26)

If you look at Genesis 1:26, it says, *"Then God said, 'Let Us make man in Our image…'"* Here, 'Us' signifies the Triune God—the Father, the Son, and the Holy Spirit. Although each of the roles of the Father, Son, and Holy Spirit in making man and fulfilling the providence of salvation is different, because the Three are one by origin, They are called God the Trinity or the Triune God.

This is a very important doctrine of the Christian faith, and because it is the secret message about the origin of the Creator God, it is difficult to fully grasp this concept with man's limited logic and knowledge. However, in order to solve the problem of sin and receive complete salvation, we need to have the correct knowledge about the Trinity of God the Father, God the Son, and God the Holy Spirit. Only when we have this understanding, can we fully enjoy the blessing and authority of being God's children.

Who is the Father God?

Above all else, God is the Creator of the universe. Genesis chapter 1 depicts how God created the universe. From complete nothingness, God created the heavens and the earth in six days with His Word. Then on the sixth day, God created Adam, the father of mankind. Just by looking at the order and harmony of everything in creation, we can know that God is alive, and that there is one Creator God.

God is omniscient. God is perfect and He knows everything. Therefore, He lets us know about future events by prophecy through those people who have close fellowships with Him (Amos 3:7). God is also omnipotent and can do anything. That is why the Bible holds a record of countless signs and wonders that cannot be accomplished by man's power and ability.

Also, God exists on His own. In Exodus chapter 3 we come across the scene where God appears to Moses. In a burning bush God calls him to become the leader of the Exodus from Egypt. At this time, He tells Moses, *"I AM WHO I AM."* He was explaining one of His characteristics, which is His self-existence. This means that no one created, nor gave birth to God. He existed on His own from before the beginning.

God is also the author of the Bible. But, because the Creator God far exceeds man, it is hard to fully explain His existence from man's perspective. This is because God is an infinite being; therefore, with limited insight, man can not completely know everything about Him.

In the Bible, we can see that the Father God is called differently, depending on the situation. In Exodus 6:3 it says, *"And I appeared to Abraham, Isaac, and Jacob, as God Almighty, but by My name, LORD, I did not make Myself known to them."* And in Exodus 15:3, it is written, *"The LORD is a warrior; the LORD is His name."* The name 'LORD' not only means 'the one who self exists'; but it also means the one and only true God who rules over all the nations of the world, and everything in it.

And the expression 'God' is used with the meaning that He abides with each race, country, or individual; therefore this name is used to show God's humanity. While the name 'LORD' is the broader, more public name for the Godhead, 'God' is the expression for God's humanity who has a close, spiritual fellowship with each individual person. "The God of Abraham, the God of Isaac, and the God of Jacob" is such an example.

So why do we call this God the 'Father God'? This is because God is not only the governor of the entire universe and the ultimate Judge; but most importantly, He is the supreme director over the planning and execution of the cultivation of man. If we believe in this God, we can call Him 'Father', and experience the amazing power and blessing of being His children.

Father God: the supreme director of human cultivation

The Creator God began human cultivation in order to gain true children with whom He could share a true, loving relationship. But as there is a beginning and an end to all created things, there is a beginning and an end for the earthly life of man.

Revelations 20:11-15 says, *"Then I saw a great white throne and Him who sat upon it, from whose presence earth and heaven fled away, and no place was found for them. And I saw the dead, the great and the small, standing before the throne, and books were opened; and another book was opened, which is the book of life; and the dead were judged from the things which were written in the books, according to their deeds. And the sea gave up the dead which were in it, and death and Hades gave up the dead which were in them; and they were judged, every one of them according to their deeds. Then death and Hades were thrown into the lake of fire. This is the second death, the lake of fire. And if anyone's name was not found written in the book of life, he was thrown into the lake of fire."*

This passage is an explanation of the Great White Throne Judgment. When the cultivation of man ends here on earth, the Lord will return in the air to take all the believers. Then, those believers who are living will be lifted up into the Air, where the Seven-Year Wedding Banquet will take place. While the Wedding Banquet is going on in the Air, there will be seven years of tribulation here on Earth. After that, the Lord will return to Earth and reign over it for a millennium. And after the millennium, will be the Great White Throne Judgment. At this time, the children of God, whose names are recorded in the book of life, will go to Heaven, and those whose names are not recorded in the book of life will be judged according to their deeds and then go to Hell.

When we look at the Bible, we can see that from the moment God created man to this day, God loves us just the same. Even after Adam and Eve sinned and were exiled from the Garden of Eden, God let us know about His will, His providence, and the things to come through righteous men like Noah, Abraham, Moses, David, and Daniel. Even today, God's power and presence are still evident in our lives. He works through those people who truly acknowledge Him, and love Him.

When we look at the Old Testament, we can see that because God loves us, He teaches us how not to fall into sin and how to live in righteousness. He teaches us what sin and righteousness are so that we can avoid judgment. He also teaches us that as we worship Him, we should set aside special festivities to make sacrifices to Him so we do not forget the living God. We can see that He blessed those who believed in Him, and for those who sinned, He gave them a chance to turn away from their sin—either through punishment or some other way. He also used His prophets to reveal His will, and to teach us to live in the truth.

However, people did not obey, but rather they continued to sin. In order to solve this problem, He sent the Savior, Jesus Christ, whom He had prepared since before the ages. And, it was He who opened the way of salvation so that all people could be saved through faith.

Who is the Son, Jesus Christ?

A person who has committed a sin cannot atone for another person's sin, so a person without any sin was needed. This is why God Himself had to put on the flesh and come into this world—and this was Jesus. Because the wages of sin is death, Jesus had to receive the execution on the cross in order to atone for our sin. This is because without the shedding of blood, there is no forgiveness of sin (Leviticus 17:11; Hebrews 9:22).

Under God's providence, Jesus died on a wooden cross in order to free mankind from being under the curse of the law. After redeeming the mankind from their sins, He rose from the dead on the third day. Therefore anyone who believes in Jesus Christ as their Savior is forgiven of their sins and receives salvation. Just like Jesus, who became the first fruit of the resurrection, we too, will resurrect and enter into Heaven.

In John 14:6 Jesus says, *"I am the way, and the truth, and the life; no one comes to the Father but through Me."* Jesus is the way because He became the way for mankind to enter into Heaven where the Father God reigns; He is the truth because He is the Word of God that became flesh and came into this world; and, He is the life because it is through Him alone that man receives salvation and eternal life.

While He was here on earth, Jesus obeyed the Law completely. In accordance with the laws of Israel, He was circumcised on the eighth day of His birth. He lived with His parents until the age of 30 and fulfilled all of His duties. Jesus had neither original sin nor committed sins. Therefore it is written about Jesus in 1 Peter 2:22, *"...who committed no sin, nor was any deceit found in His mouth."*

A short time later, according to God's will, Jesus began fasting for 40 days before setting out to fulfill His ministry. He told many people about the living God and the gospel of the kingdom of heaven, and He showed God's power wherever He went. He clearly showed that God is the true god, and that He is the supreme overseer of life and death.

The reason Jesus came into this world was to tell all mankind about the Father God, to destroy the enemy devil, to save us from sin and lead us to the way of eternal life. So in John 4:34, Jesus says, *"My food is to do the will of Him who sent Me and to accomplish His work."*

Jesus Christ the Savior

Jesus Christ is not just one of the four greatest philosophers that the world has ever known. He is the Savior that opened the way of salvation for all mankind; therefore He cannot be placed on the same level as men, who are mere creations. If you look at Philippians 2:6-11 it says, *"Who, although He existed in the form of God, did not regard equality with God a thing to be grasped, but emptied Himself, taking the form of a bondservant, and being made in the likeness of men. Being found in appearance as a man, He humbled Himself by becoming obedient to the point of death, even death on a cross. For this reason also, God highly exalted Him, and bestowed on Him the name which is above every name, so that at the name of Jesus every knee will bow, of those who are in heaven and on earth and under the earth, and that every tongue will confess that Jesus Christ is Lord, to the glory of God the Father."*

Because Jesus obeyed God and sacrificed Himself in accordance with God's will, God lifted Him up to the utmost place at His right hand, and named Him the King of kings and the Lord of lords.

Who is the Holy Spirit, the Helper?

When Jesus was here in this world, He had to work within the limitations of time and space because He had the human body. He spread the gospel in the regions of Judea, Samaria, and Galilee, but He could not spread the gospel to more distant regions. However, after Jesus resurrected and ascended into Heaven, He sent us the Holy Spirit, the Helper, who would come upon all mankind transcending limitations of time and space.

The definition of "helper" is: 'a prophet who defends, persuades, or helps another realize his wrong'; 'a counselor who encourages and strengthens another'.

Being holy and one with God, the Holy Spirit knows even the depths of God's heart (1 Corinthians 2:10). As a sinner cannot see God, in the same way the Holy Spirit cannot dwell in a sinner. So before Jesus redeemed us by dying on the cross and shedding His blood for us, the Holy Spirit could not come into our hearts.

But after Jesus died and then resurrected, the problem of sin was resolved and anyone who opens his heart and accepts Jesus Christ could then receive the Holy Spirit. When one is justified by faith, God gives them the gift of the Holy Spirit so that the Holy Spirit might then dwell in his or her heart. The Holy Spirit leads us and guides us, and through Him, we can communicate with God.

Then why does God give His children the gift of the Holy Spirit? This is because unless the Holy Spirit comes to us and revives our spirit—which was dead due to Adam's sin—we cannot enter into the truth, or dwell in the truth. When we believe in Jesus Christ and receive the Holy Spirit, the Holy Spirit comes into our hearts and teaches us God's laws, which is the Truth, so that we may live according to these laws and dwell in the truth.

The Work of the Holy Spirit, the Helper

The primary work of the Holy Spirit is the work for us to be born again. By being born again, we realize God's laws and try to abide by them. This is why Jesus said, *"Unless one is born of water and the Spirit he cannot enter into the kingdom of God. That which is born of the flesh is flesh, and that which is born of the Spirit is spirit"* (John 3:5-6). So unless we are born again of water and the Holy Spirit, we cannot receive salvation.

Here, water refers to the living water—God's Word. We need to become totally cleansed and transformed by God's Word, or the truth. So what does it mean to be born again of the Holy Spirit? When we accept Jesus Christ, God gives us the gift of the Holy Spirit and acknowledges us as His children (Acts 2:38). Children of God who receive the Holy Spirit listen to the Word of truth and learn to distinguish between good and evil. And when they pray wholeheartedly, God gives them the grace and strength to live according to His Word. This is being born again of the Holy Spirit. And depending on the extent to which the Spirit gives birth to spirit for each individual, he or she is transformed by the truth. And depending on the extent to which the individual is changed by the truth, that's how much he can receive spiritual faith from God.

Secondly, the Holy Spirit helps our weaknesses and intercedes for us with groanings too deep for words, so that we can pray (Romans 8:26). He also breaks us to make better vessels of us. And, just as Jesus said, *"But the Helper, the Holy Spirit, whom the Father will send in My name, He will teach you all things, and bring to your remembrance all that I said to you"* (John 14:26), the Holy Spirit guides us into the truth and teaches us about the events to come in the future (John 16:13).

Furthermore, when we obey the desires of the Holy Spirit, He lets us bear fruit and receive spiritual gifts. So if we receive the Holy Spirit and act according to the truth, He works within us so we can bear the fruits of love, joy, peace, patience, kindness, goodness, faithfulness, gentleness, and self-control (Galatians 5:22-23). Not only that, He also gives gifts that are beneficial to us in our spiritual lives as believers, such as words of wisdom, words of knowledge, faith, gifts of healing, the effecting of miracles, prophecy, the distinguishing of spirits, various kinds of tongues, and the interpretation of tongues (1 Corinthians 12:7-10).

Moreover, the Spirit also speaks to us (Acts 10:19), gives us commands (Acts 8:29), and at times forbids us to take action if it goes against God's will (Acts 16:6).

God the Trinity fulfills the providence of salvation

So the Father, the Son, and the Holy Spirit were all originally one. In the beginning, this one God, existing as Light with the chiming voice within, governed the entire universe (John 1:1; 1 John 1:5). Then, at a certain point, in order to gain true children with whom He could share His love, He began to plan for the providence of human cultivation. He divided the one space in which He originally resided into many spaces, and began to exist as the Triune God.

God the Son, Jesus Christ was begotten of the Original God (Acts 13:33; Hebrews 5:5), and God the Holy Spirit, was also begotten from the Original God (John 15:26; Galatians 4:6). Therefore God the Father, God the Son, and God the Holy Spirit – the Triune God have been fulfilling the providence of mankind's salvation, and will continue to fulfill it together until the day of the Great White Throne Judgment.

When Jesus was hung on the cross, He was not suffering by Himself. The Father God and the Holy Spirit also experienced the pain with Him. Also, as the Holy Spirit fulfills His ministry mourning and interceding for the souls here on earth, the Father God and the Lord are working with Him as well.

In 1 John 5:7-8 it says, *"For there are three that testify: the Spirit and the water and the blood; and the three are in agreement."* The water spiritually symbolizes the ministry of God's Word, and the blood spiritually symbolizes the ministry of the Lord and the shedding of His blood on the cross. By working together in Their ministries, God the Trinity gives evidence of salvation to all the believers.

Also, Matthew 28:19 says, *"Go therefore and make disciples of all the nations, baptizing them in the name of the Father and the Son and the Holy Spirit."* And 2 Corinthians 13:14 reads, *"The grace of the Lord Jesus Christ, and the love of God, and the fellowship of the Holy Spirit, be with you all."* We can see here people are baptized and blessed in the name of God the Trinity.

In this way, because the God Father, God the Son, and God the Holy Spirit are of one nature, one heart, and one mind by origin, each of Their roles in the cultivation of man are distinguished in an orderly way. God clearly distinguished the Old Testament period, where God the Father Himself was leading His people; the New Testament period, where Jesus came into this world to become the Savior for mankind; and the latter period of grace, where the Holy Spirit, the Helper, carries out His ministry. God the Trinity has been fulfilling His will in each of those periods respectively.

Acts 2:38 says, *"Repent, and each of you be baptized in the name of Jesus Christ for the forgiveness of your sins; and you will receive the gift of the Holy Spirit."* And, as it is written in 2 Corinthians 1:22, *"Who [God] also sealed us and gave us the Spirit in our hearts as a pledge,"* if we accept Jesus Christ and receive the Holy Spirit, we not only receive the right to become God's children (John 1:12), but we can also receive the guidance of the Holy Spirit to cast out sin and live in the Light. When our soul prospers, all things will prosper, and we receive the blessing of both spiritual and physical health. And once we get to Heaven, we also enjoy eternal life!

If God the Father existed alone, we could not receive

salvation wholly. We need Jesus Christ because we can only enter God's kingdom after being washed of our sins. And if we are to cast off our sins and seek after God's image, we need the help of the Holy Spirit. Because God the Trinity—the Father, the Son, and the Holy Spirit—helps us, we can receive complete salvation and give glory to God.

Glossary

Flesh and the works of the flesh

The term 'flesh' from a spiritual perspective is a general term that refers to the untruth in our hearts that comes out into the open as actions. For example, hate, envy, adultery, pride, and the like, coming out into specific actions such as violence, abuse, murder, etc., are collectively called "the flesh", and each of these sins, when classified individually, are called "works of the flesh".

Lust of the flesh, lust of the eyes, boastful pride of life

"Lust of the flesh" refers to the natures that cause men to commit sins following the desires of flesh. These tendencies include hate, pride, rage, laziness, adultery, etc. When these sinful natures encounter a certain environment that provokes them, lust of the flesh begins to come out. For example, if someone has the sinful nature of 'judging and condemning' others, he or she will like to hear rumors and enjoy gossiping.

"Lust of the eyes" refers to the sinful nature that makes a person desire things of the flesh when the heart is provoked by the senses of seeing and hearing through the eyes and ears. The lust of the eyes is stimulated as we see and hear things of this world. If these things are not cast out but if we continue to receive and input them, the lust of the flesh is provoked, and we end up committing sin.

"Boastful pride of life" refers to the sinful nature in a man that makes him want to show himself off by boasting or bragging while following the pleasures of this world. If a person has this sinful nature, he will constantly strive to gain things of this world in order to show himself off.

Chapter 3

Works of the Flesh

> *"Now the works of the flesh are evident, which are: adultery, fornication, uncleanness, lewdness, idolatry, sorcery, hatred, contentions, jealousies, outbursts of wrath, selfish ambitions, dissensions, heresies, envy, murders, drunkenness, revelries, and the like; of which I tell you beforehand, just as I also told you in time past, that those who practice such things will not inherit the kingdom of God."*
> (Galatians 5:19-21, NKJV)

Even Christians who have been believers for a long time may be unfamiliar with the term "works of the flesh". This is because in many cases churches do not teach about sin concretely. However, as clearly as it is written in Matthew 7:21, *"Not everyone who says to Me, 'Lord, Lord,' will enter the kingdom of heaven, but he who does the will of My Father who is in heaven will enter,"* we need to know exactly what God's will is, and we definitely need to know about the sins that God hates.

God not only calls visible wrong deeds "sins", but He also considers hate, envy, jealousy, judging and/or condemning others, callousness, a lying heart, etc. as sins as well. According to the Bible, "Whatever is not from faith" (Romans 14:23), knowing the right thing to do and not doing it (James 4:17), not doing the good that I want to do, and instead practicing the evil that I do not want (Romans 7:19-20), deeds of the flesh (Galatians 5:19-21), and things of the flesh (Romans 8:5) are all called "sins".

All these kinds of sins form a wall that stands between us and God, as it is written in Isaiah 59:1-3, *"Behold, the LORD's hand is not so short that it cannot save; nor is His ear so dull that it cannot hear. But your iniquities have made a separation between you and your God, and your sins have hidden His face from you so that He does not hear. For your hands are defiled with blood and your fingers with iniquity; your lips have spoken falsehood, your tongue mutters wickedness."*

So what specific walls of sin stand between us and God?

Things of the flesh and works of the flesh

Normally, when referring to the human body, the words "body" and "flesh" are used interchangeably. However, the spiritual definition of the "flesh" is different. Galatians 5:24 says, *"Now those who belong to Christ Jesus have crucified the flesh with its passions and desires."* Now this does not mean we have literally crucified our bodies.

We need to know the spiritual meaning of the word "flesh" to understand the meaning of the above verse. Not all uses of the word "flesh" have a spiritual meaning. Sometimes they simply refer to the human body. This is why we need to know this term more clearly, so we can see when the word is used with the spiritual connotation and when it is not.

Originally, man was created with a spirit, a soul, and a body, and he had no sin. However, after disobeying God's Word, man became a sinner. And, since the wages of sin is death (Romans 6:23), the spirit, which is the master of the man, died. And the human body became a futile thing which, with the passing of time, eventually becomes decrepit, decays, and returns to a handful of dust. And so man holds sin within his body, and through actions he commits these sins. This is where the word "flesh" comes in.

The "flesh", as a spiritual term, represents the combination of sinful natures and the human body from which the truth leaked out. So when the Bible refers to the "flesh", it signifies the sin which has not yet come out into action, but which could be induced at any given moment. This includes sinful thoughts, and all other types of sins within our body. And all of these sins, when labeled collectively, are called "things of the flesh".

In other words, hate, pride, rage, judging, condemning, adultery, greed, etc., are collectively called "flesh", and each of these sins individually is called a "thing of the flesh". So as long as these things of the flesh remain in one's heart, under the right circumstances, they can come out into the open at any given time as sinful actions. For example, if there is a deceitful nature in one's heart, it may not be so evident under normal circumstances, but if one is pressed into an adverse, or urgent situation, he or she may lie to another person through deceitful words or actions.

Sins that come out into the open like this are also of the "flesh", but each of the sins committed in action is called a "work of the flesh". If, for example, you have a desire to hit someone, this 'ill desire' is considered a "thing of the flesh". And if you actually hit someone, this is then considered a "work of the flesh".

If you look at Genesis 6:3, it says, *"Then the LORD said, 'My Spirit shall not strive with man forever, because he also is flesh.'"* God is stating that He would no longer strive with man forever, for man had turned into flesh. Then does this mean that God is not with us? No, it does not. Because we have accepted Jesus Christ, received the Holy Spirit, and been born again as God's children, we are no longer men of flesh.

If we live according to God's Words and follow the guidance of the Holy Spirit, the Spirit gives birth to spirit, and we become transformed into men of spirit. God, who is spirit, dwells with those who are transforming every day into men of spirit. However, God does not dwell with those people who say they believe, and yet continue to sin and commit works of the flesh. The Bible points out over and over again, how these kinds of people cannot receive salvation (Psalm 92:7; Matthew 7:21; Romans 6:23).

Works of the flesh that keep man from inheriting the kingdom of God

If, after living in the midst of sin, we realize we are sinners and accept Jesus Christ, we try not to commit works of the flesh that blatantly appear as 'sins'. Yes, God is not pleased with 'things of the flesh', but it is the 'works of the flesh' that can actually keep us from inheriting the kingdom of God. Therefore, we must try all the more never to commit works of the flesh.

1 John 3:4 says, *"Everyone who practices sin also practices lawlessness; and sin is lawlessness."* Here, *"Everyone who practices sin"* is anyone who commits works of the flesh. Also, unrighteousness is lawlessness; therefore if you are unrighteous, even if you say you are a believer, the Bible warns that you cannot receive salvation.

1 Corinthians 6:9-10 states, *"Or do you not know that the unrighteous will not inherit the kingdom of God? Do not be deceived; neither fornicators, nor idolaters, nor adulterers, nor effeminate, nor homosexuals, nor thieves, nor the covetous, nor drunkards, nor revilers, nor swindlers, will inherit the kingdom of God."*

Matthew chapter 13 clearly explains what will happen to these kinds of people at the end of the age: *"The Son of Man will send forth His angels, and they will gather out of His kingdom all stumbling blocks, and those who commit lawlessness, and will throw them into the furnace of fire; in that place there will be weeping and gnashing of teeth."* (vv. 41-42). Why would this happen? This is because instead of trying to cast out sin, these people lived a life of compromising with the untruth of this world. So in God's eyes, they are not 'wheat', but 'chaff'.

So it is most important that we first figure out what kind of walls of sin we have built up between God and us, and we need to break down that wall. Only after we solve this sin problem can we be acknowledged by God as having faith, and we can grow and mature as 'wheat'. And this is when we can receive the answers to our prayers, and experience healing and blessings.

Evident works of the flesh

Since works of the flesh come out as actions, we can clearly see the depraved and corrupt image of the sin committed. The most evident works of the flesh are immorality, impurity and sensuality. These sins are sexual sins, and those committing these types of sins cannot receive salvation. Therefore, anyone that these sins apply to must quickly repent and turn back from these ways.

1) Immorality, impurity, **sensuality**

First, 'immorality' here refers to sexual immorality. It is when an unmarried man and woman have a physical relationship with one another. In this day and age, because our society is so full of sin, having sexual relations before marriage has become a norm. However, even if two people are going to be wed, and they love each other, this is still considered acting in untruth. But nowadays, people are not even ashamed. They don't even consider such action a sin. This is because through dramas or movies, society turns stories of unlawful affairs and relationships that deviate from the truth into 'beautiful love stories'. As people watch and become involved in these types of dramas and movies, their sense of discretion about sin dims, and little by little, people become totally desensitized to sin.

Sexual immorality is not acceptable even from an ethical or moral standpoint. So how much more unacceptable would it be in the eyes of the holy God? If two people truly love one another, they should first, through the institution of marriage, receive acknowledgement from God, and from their parents and relatives, and then leave their parents and become one flesh.

Secondly, sexual immorality is when a married man or woman does not keep their marriage vow sacred. Namely, this is when a husband or a wife indulges in a relationship with someone other than their lawful spouse. However, aside from the adultery that occurs in the relationships between people, there is also a spiritual adultery that people often commit. This is when people call themselves believers, and yet they worship idols or consult with a psychic or a sorcerer, or depend on some sort of black magic or wicked enchantments. This is the act of worshipping evil spirits and demons.

If you look at Numbers chapter 25, while the sons of Israel were staying in Shittim, the people not only committed immorality with the women of Moab; they also bowed down to their gods. As a result, God's wrath was upon them, and 24,000 people died from a plague in one day. Therefore, if someone says he or she believes in God, and yet depends on idols and demons, this is the act of spiritual adultery, and the act of betraying God.

Next, 'impurity' is when any sinful nature goes too far and becomes filthy. For example, when an adulterous heart goes too far, a robber may rape both a mother and her daughter at the same time. When jealousy has gone too far, it can also become 'impurity'. For example, if a person becomes jealous of another person to the point of drawing a picture of that person and throwing darts at the picture, or pricking the picture with needles, such abnormal acts come out as the result of that jealousy, and these acts are of 'impurity'.

Before one believes in God, he or she may have the sinful

natures of hate, jealousy, or adultery in them. Because of Adam's original sin, every man is born with untruth, which is at the root of every man's nature. When these sinful natures inside of a man cross a certain limit and goes beyond the confines of morals and ethics and causes damage and pain to another person, we say it is 'impure'.

'Sensuality' is seeking pleasure in sensual things, such as sexual desires or fantasies, and committing all kinds of indecent acts while following these lustful desires. 'Sensuality' is different from 'adultery' in that a person lives most of his daily life drenched in adulterous thoughts, words, and or actions. For example, mating with an animal, or having homosexual relations – a woman committing indecent acts with another woman, or a man with another man – or using sex tools, etc. are all evil acts that fall under 'sensuality'.

In today's society, people say homosexuals should receive respect. However, this goes against God and against rationality (Romans 1:26-27). Also, men who consider themselves as women, or women who think of themselves as men, or transsexuals, are not acceptable to God (Deuteronomy 22:5). This goes against God's order of creation.

When society begins to corrupt due to sin, the first thing that becomes disorderly is the people's morals and ethics regarding sex. Historically, whenever a society's sex culture became corrupt, it was followed by God's judgment. Sodom and Gomorrah and Pompeii are very good examples of this. When we see how our society's sex culture is becoming disorderly all over the world – to the point it cannot be restored – we can know that the Day of Judgment is near.

2) Idolatry, sorcery, and enmity

'Idols' can be divided into two major categories. The first is creating an image of a god that has no shape by forming some physical shape for it, or making some kind of image and making it an object of worship. People want things that they can see with their eyes, touch with their hands, and feel with their flesh. That is why people use wood, rocks, steel, gold, or silver to create images of man, animals, birds, or fish to worship it. Or they give some name, like the god of the sun, moon, and stars, and worship it (Deuteronomy 4:16-19). This is called 'idolatry'.

In Exodus chapter 32, we see that when Moses went up to Mount Sinai to receive the Law and didn't come back down right away, the Israelites made a golden calf and worshipped it. Even though they saw numerous signs and wonders, they still wouldn't believe, and finally, they began worshipping an idol. Seeing this, God's wrath was upon them, and He said He would destroy them. At that time, their lives were spared thanks to Moses' fervent prayer. But as a result of this event, those who were over twenty years of age at the Exodus could not enter the land of Canaan, and they died in the desert. From this, we can see just how much God hates the act of making idols, bowing to them, or worshipping them.

Secondly, if there is something we love more than God, then that becomes an idol. Colossians 3:5-6 reads, *"Therefore consider the members of your earthly body as dead to immorality, impurity, passion, evil desire, and greed, which amounts to idolatry. For it is because of these things that the wrath of God will come upon the sons of disobedience."*

For example, if someone has greed in his heart, then he might love material possessions more than God and in order to make more money he may not keep the Lord's Day holy. Also, if a person tries to satisfy the greed in his heart by loving other people or things more than God—like his spouse, children, fame, power, knowledge, entertainment, television, sports, hobbies, or dating—and does not like to pray and lead a fervent spiritual life, this is the act of idol worship.

Just because God told us not to commit idol worship, if some people ask, "So does God want us to *only* worship *Him* and love *Him*?" and they think God is selfish, they are under a misconception. God did not tell us to love Him first in order to be a dictator. He did this to guide us to live lives worthy of being human beings. If a person loves and worships other things more than God, he cannot fulfill his duties as a human being, and he cannot cast out sin from his life.

Next, the dictionary defines 'sorcery' as "the practices or spells of a person who is supposed to exercise supernatural powers or enchantments through the aid of evil spirits; black magic; witchery." Consulting with shamans, psychics, and the like, all fall into this category. Some people go to see a shaman or a psychic to ask about their child who's getting ready to take a college entrance exam, or to find out if their fiancé is the right match. Or if some trouble arises in their household, they try to get an amulet or a charm for good luck. But children of God should never do these kinds of things, because doing these things will bring evil spirits into their lives and greater tribulations will occur as a result.

'Enchantments' and 'spells' are tactics for deceiving others, like devising evil plans to swindle someone, or make them fall into a trap. From a spiritual perspective, 'sorcery' is the act of tricking another person through crafty deceptions. This is why darkness rules in all different parts of our society today.

'Enmity' is a feeling of resentment or hostility against someone and wishing for his or her ultimate ruin. If you carefully study the heart of the people who have enmity with another person, you can see that they actually distance themselves and hate the other person either because they don't like that person for some reason, or because of their own evil emotions. Now when these evil emotions grow past a certain limit, they can explode into actions that can bring harm to the other person; such as creating calumnies against them, gossiping and slandering about them, and all kinds of other maliciously evil deeds.

In Samuel chapter 16, we see that as soon as the spirit of the LORD left Saul, evil spirits came to bother him. But when David played on his harp, Saul was refreshed and well, and the evil spirits left him. Also, David killed the Philistine giant, Goliath, with a sling and stone and saved the nation of Israel from a crisis, putting his life on the line to be faithful to Saul. However, Saul was afraid of his reign being taken by David, and he spent many years chasing David to kill him. Finally, God disowned Saul. God's Word tells us to even love our enemies. Therefore we should never have enmity with anyone.

3) Strife, jealousy, outbursts of anger

'Strife' occurs when people set their own personal gain and

power as priority before others and fight for it. Contention usually begins with greed and causes conflicts that lead to strife between national leaders, political party members, family members, people within the church, and in all other interpersonal relationships.

In Korean history we have an example of strife between national leaders. Dae Won Goon, the father of the last emperor of the Chosun Dynasty and his daughter-in-law Empress Myong Sung were having dispute over political power against each other with different foreign powers backing each of them. It lasted more than ten years. This led to national chaos, which in turn led to a rebellion with military insurrection and even a farmers' revolution. Many political leaders were killed as a result, and the Empress Myong Sung was also killed by the hands of Japanese assassins. Ultimately, due to this dispute between key national leaders, Korea lost its sovereignty to the Japanese.

Contentions may also occur between husband and wife, or parent and child. If both spouses want the other person to heed to *their* wishes, this can cause strife and even lead to separation. There are even cases where spouses sue each other and become life-long enemies. If there is contention in the church, Satan's work begins and prevents the church from growing, and keeping all the departments of the church from functioning correctly.

As we read through the Bible, we frequently come across scenes where there are conflicts and contentions. In 2 Samuel 18:7, we see that David's son, Absalom, led a rebellion against David, and twenty thousand men were killed, all in one day. Also, after the death of Solomon, Israel divided into the northern kingdom of Israel and the southern kingdom of Judah, and even after that, strife and war continued on and on. Especially in the northern kingdom of Israel, the throne was constantly threatened by contention. So, knowing that contentions lead to pain and destruction, I hope that you will always seek for the benefit of others and make peace.

Next, 'jealousy' is when a person distances himself from other individuals and hates them because he has become envious of them thinking that they are better than he is. When jealousy grows, it can develop into anger filled with evil. This might cause contentions which leads to disputes.

If you refer to the Bible, Jacob's two wives, Leah and Rachel, were jealous of each other, with Jacob between them (Genesis chapter 30). King Saul was jealous of David, who was given more love from the people than he received (1 Samuel 18:7-8). Cain was jealous of his brother, Abel, and killed him (Genesis 4:1-8). Jealousy arises from the evil in a person's heart that provokes them to satisfy his or her greed.

The easiest way to discover if you have jealousy is to see if you ever feel uncomfortable when another person thrives and does well. Furthermore, you may start to dislike the other person and want to take what they have. Also, if you ever compare yourself with another person and feel discouraged, jealousy is at the root of this problem. When that person is of similar age, faith, experience, and background or environment it is particularly easy to feel jealous of that person. Just as God commanded us to "love your neighbor as yourself", if another person is complimented because they are better than us at something, God wants us to be joyful with them. He wants us to be joyful as if we were receiving the compliment ourselves.

'Outbursts of anger' is expressions of anger that go beyond just getting angry in the inside and trying to hold it in. They oftentimes have devastating results. They are, for example, easily getting angry whenever something does not agree with your own opinion or thoughts and using violence, and even killing. Simply becoming frustrated and expressing that frustration does not hinder salvation; however, if you have the evil nature of rage, you may act with outbursts of wrath. Therefore, you must pull out this evil at its roots and cast it away.

This is the case of King Saul, who had become jealous of David and persistently tried to kill him just because he received praise from the people—praise which he deserved! There are several places in the Bible where Saul displayed outbursts of anger. He once threw a spear at David (1 Samuel 18:1). Just because the city of Nob helped David on the run, Saul struck the city down. It was the city of the priests, and Saul not only had men, women, children and infants killed; he also struck down the oxen, donkeys, and sheep (1 Samuel 22:19). If we become overly angry like this, we are heaping up a great amount of sin.

4) Disputes, dissensions, factions

'Disputes' causes people to be separated. If something does not befit them, they form clicks or groups. It does not simply refer to people that are close, share something in common, or meet frequently. These are adverse groups where its members gossip, criticize, judge and condemn. These groups can form within a family, in the neighborhood, and even in the church.

If, for example, someone does not like his or her ministers and begins gossiping about them with a circle of people that have the same opinion, then this is the 'synagogue of Satan'. Because these people are hindering the ministers by judging and condemning them, the church they serve cannot experience revival.

'Dissensions' are creating a faction and separating oneself from the rest while following his own will and thoughts. An example is creating a division within the church. This is an act that goes against the good will of God, as it is caused by a strong opinion that one's thinking is the only right way of thinking, and everything must be tailored to meet with one's own benefit.

David's son, Absalom betrayed and rebelled against his father (2 Samuel chapter 15), because he was following his greed. During this rebellion, many Israelites, even Ahitophel, David's counselor, sided with Absalom and betrayed David. God forsakes men like these that engage in works of the flesh. Therefore, Absalom and all the men that sided with him were ultimately defeated and faced miserable ends.

'Heresy' is the act of people denying the Lord, who bought them, bringing swift destruction upon themselves (2 Peter 2:1). Jesus Christ shed His blood to save us, while we were in the midst of sin; therefore it is right to say that He bought us with His blood. So if we claim to believe in God but deny the Holy Trinity, or deny Jesus Christ who bought us with His blood, then it is like we are bringing destruction upon ourselves.

There are times when, without knowing the true definition of heresy, people accuse and condemn other people of heresy just because they are a little different from themselves. However, this is a very dangerous thing to do, and it can fall into the category of hindering the work of the Holy Spirit. If someone believes in the Trinity God—Father, Son, and Holy Spirit, and does not deny Jesus Christ, we cannot condemn them of heresy.

5) Envy, murders, drunkenness, revelries

'Envy' is jealousy displayed into actions. Jealousy is to disapprove or dislike others when things go well with them, and envy is a step further out where this disapproval provokes someone to carry out actions that bring harm to others. Normally, envy can be found most often among women, but it can most certainly occur among men; and if it progresses, it can lead to grave sins like murder. And even if it doesn't progress to the point of murder, it can go as far as intimidating or hurting the other person, or other evil actions such as conspiring against another person or people.

Next, there is 'drunkenness'. In the Bible, there is a scene after the judgment of the flood, where Noah drank wine, became drunk, and made a mistake. Noah's drunkenness ultimately caused Noah to curse his second son, who brought his weakness out into the open. Ephesians 5:18 says, *"And do not get drunk with wine, for that is dissipation, but be filled with the Spirit."* This means that drunkenness is a sin.

The reason why the Bible has record of people drinking wine is because Israel has many dry areas of wilderness, and water is very scarce. Therefore, alternative wine drinks made from the pure juice of grapes, and other fruits high in sweet concentrates were permitted (Deuteronomy 14:26). However, the people of

Israel drank this wine in place of water; but not enough to get drunk from it. But in our country nowadays, where water for drinking is very plentiful, we really don't have the need to drink wine or alcohol.

In the Bible, we can see that God did not intend for believers to drink strong drinks like wine (Leviticus 10:9; Romans 14:21). Proverbs 31:4-6 reads: *"It is not for kings, O Lemuel, it is not for kings to drink wine, or for rulers to desire strong drink, for they will drink and forget what is decreed, and pervert the rights of all the afflicted. Give strong drink to him who is perishing, and wine to him whose life is bitter."*

You may say, "Isn't it okay to drink just enough, but not enough to get drunk?" But even if you drink a little, you're getting 'just a little bit drunk'. You're still getting drunk even if it is 'only a little'. When you get drunk, you lose self-control, so even if you are normally a calm and gentle person, you may become violent when you're drunk. There are people who begin speaking crudely and acting roughly, or even cause a scene. Also, because getting drunk causes lack of rationality and discretion, some people can end up committing all kinds of different sins. It's very common to see people ruining their health from heavy drinking, and people who become alcoholics bring pain not only upon themselves, but also upon the lives of their loved ones. But in many cases, even though people know how harmful drinking can be, once they start, they can't stop, and they continue to drink and ruin their lives. This is why 'drunkenness' is included in the list of 'works of the flesh'.

Several things fall under the category of "Revelries". If

someone is so engrossed in drinking, gaming, gambling, and the like, that he cannot tend to his responsibilities as head of household, or care for a child as a parent, then God considers this as 'revelry'. Also, not having self-control and chasing after sexual pleasures and leading an immoral lifestyle, or living any way you want also falls under 'revelry'.

Another problem in today's society is people's obsession over superficial luxury products and brand names that cause them to become involved with revelries. People buy designer handbags, clothing, shoes, etc. that they can't afford using their credit cards, and this leads to huge debt. Not having a way to pay back the debt, some people even commit crimes or commit suicide. This is the case of people not having self-control over their greed, chasing after revelries, and then having to pay the consequences.

6) And the like…

God tells us that there are many other works of the flesh aside from the ones that were already mentioned. However, thinking, 'How can I ever get rid of all these sins?' we should not give up at the very start. Even if you have many sins, if you make a strong commitment in your heart and try hard, you can definitely get rid of those sins. While trying not to commit works of the flesh, if you work hard to do good deeds, and pray continuously, you will receive the grace of God and gain the power to transform. This may be impossible with man's power; but anything is possible with God's power (Mark 10:27).

What happens if you live like the worldly people in the midst of sin and revelries even though you have heard and known that you cannot inherit the kingdom of God if you keep on committing works of the flesh? Then you are a man of flesh, namely 'chaff,' and you cannot receive salvation. 1 Corinthians 15:50 says, *"Now I say this, brethren, that flesh and blood cannot inherit the kingdom of God; nor does the perishable inherit the imperishable."* Also, in 1 John 3:8 says, *"The one who practices sin is of the devil; for the devil has sinned from the beginning."*

We must remember that if we commit works of the flesh and the wall of sin between God and us keeps piling up, then we cannot meet God, receive answers to our prayers, or inherit the kingdom of God, namely Heaven.

However, just because you accepted Jesus Christ and received the Holy Spirit, it does not mean you can cut off all the works of the flesh all at once. But with the help of the Holy Spirit, you need to try to live a life of holiness, and pray with the fire of the Holy Spirit. Then you can cast off works of the flesh one by one. Even if you still have a few works of the flesh you haven't been able to get rid of yet, if you try your best, God will not call you a man of flesh, but He will call you His child who became righteous by faith and He will lead you to salvation.

But this does not mean you should stay at the level of continuing to commit acts of the flesh. You need to try not only to cast off works of the flesh that are outwardly visible, but you should also try to cast off the things of the flesh that are not visible outwardly. In the Old Testament times, it was hard to cast off the things of the flesh because the Holy Spirit had not yet come and they had to do it with their own strength. Now in the New Testament times, however, we can cast out things of the flesh with the help of the Holy Spirit and become sanctified.

This is because Jesus Christ already forgave us of all of our sins by shedding His blood on the cross and sent the Holy Spirit, the Helper, to us. Therefore I pray that you will receive the help of the Holy Spirit and cast off all the works of the flesh and things of the flesh and become acknowledged as a true child of God.

Chapter 4

"Therefore Bear Fruit in Keeping with Repentance"

> *"Then Jerusalem was going out to him, and all Judea and all the district around the Jordan; and they were being baptized by him in the Jordan River, as they confessed their sins. But when he saw many of the Pharisees and Sadducees coming for baptism, he said to them, 'You brood of vipers, who warned you to flee from the wrath to come? Therefore bear fruit in keeping with repentance; and do not suppose that you can say to yourselves, "We have Abraham for our father"; for I say to you that from these stones God is able to raise up children to Abraham. The axe is already laid at the root of the trees; therefore every tree that does not bear good fruit is cut down and thrown into the fire.'"*
> (Matthew 3:5-10)

John was a prophet who was born before Jesus and who 'made the way straight for the Lord'. John knew the purpose of his life. So, when the time came, he diligently spread the news about Jesus, the coming Messiah. At that time, the Jewish people were waiting for the Messiah who would save their nation. This is why John shouted in the wilderness of Judea, *"Repent, for the kingdom of heaven is at hand!"* (Matthew 3:2) And for those who repented of their sins, he baptized them with water and guided them to accept Jesus as their Savior.

Matthew 3:11-12 says, *"As for me, I baptize you with water for repentance, but He who is coming after me is mightier than I, and I am not fit to remove His sandals; He will baptize you with the Holy Spirit and fire. His winnowing fork is in His hand, and He will thoroughly clear His threshing floor; and He will gather His wheat into the barn, but He will burn up the chaff with unquenchable fire."* John was telling people beforehand that Jesus, the Son of God who came into this world, is our Savior and will ultimately be our Judge.

When John saw many Pharisees and Sadducees coming to be baptized, he called them a "brood of vipers" and chastised them. He did this because unless they bore the proper fruit of repentance, they could not receive salvation. So, let's now take a closer look at John's rebuke to see exactly what kind of fruits we need to bear in order to receive salvation.

You brood of vipers

Both the Pharisees and the Sadducees were branches of the Judaism. The Pharisees hailed themselves as the ones that are 'set apart'. They believed in the resurrection of the righteous and the judgment of the wicked; they adhered strictly to the Law of Moses and the traditions of the elders. Therefore their status in society was significant.

On the other hand, the Sadducees were aristocratic priests

whose interests were mainly in the temple, and their views and customs were different to those of the Pharisees. They upheld the political situation under the Roman government, and they refused to believe in the resurrection, the eternal nature of the soul, angels, and spiritual beings. They even saw God's kingdom as temporal.

In Matthew 3:7, John the Baptist reproached the Pharisees and Sadducees by saying, *"You brood of vipers, who warned you to flee from the wrath to come?"* Why do you think John called them "brood of vipers", when they considered themselves believers in God?

The Pharisees and Sadducees claimed to believe in God, and they taught the Law. However, they did not recognize God's Son, Jesus. This is why Matthew 16:1-4 says, *"The Pharisees and Sadducees came up, and testing Jesus, they asked Him to show them a sign from heaven. But He replied to them, 'When it is evening, you say, "It will be fair weather, for the sky is red." And in the morning, "There will be a storm today, for the sky is red and threatening." Do you know how to discern the appearance of the sky, but cannot discern the signs of the times? An evil and adulterous generation seeks after a sign; and a sign will not be given it, except the sign of Jonah.' And He left them and went away."*

Also, Matthew 9:32-34 reads, *"As they were going out, a mute, demon-possessed man was brought to Him. After the demon was cast out, the mute man spoke; and the crowds were amazed, and were saying, 'Nothing like this has ever been seen in Israel.' But the Pharisees were saying, 'He casts out the demons by the ruler of the demons.'"* A good person would rejoice and give glory to God, since Jesus cast out a demon. But the Pharisees rather hated Jesus and judged and condemned Him, saying He was doing the work of the devil.

In Matthew chapter 12, we encounter the scene where people try to find some reason to accuse Jesus, by asking Him whether it is right or wrong to heal someone on the Sabbath. Knowing their intentions, Jesus gave them the illustration about the sheep that fell into a pit on the Sabbath to teach them that it is right to do good work on the Sabbath. He then healed a man whose hand was withered. However, instead of learning from this event, they conspired to get rid of Jesus. Because Jesus was doing things they could not do, they were jealous of Him.

1 John 3:9-10 says, *"No one who is born of God practices sin, because His seed abides in him; and he cannot sin, because he is born of God. By this the children of God and the children of the devil are obvious: anyone who does not practice righteousness is not of God, nor the one who does not love his brother."* This means that a person who commits sins is not of God.

The Pharisees and Sadducees claimed to believe in God, and yet they were full of evil. They committed things of the flesh, like jealousy, hatred, pride, and judging and condemning. They also committed other works of the flesh. They only pursued the observance and formality of the Law and sought worldly honor. They were under the influence of Satan, the old serpent (Revelations 12:9); so when John the Baptist called them 'brood of vipers', this is what he was alluding to.

Bear fruit in keeping with repentance

If we are children of God, we should be in the light because God is Light (1 John 1:5). If we are in the darkness, which is contrary to the Light, we are not children of God. If we do not act in righteousness, which is God's Word, or if we do not love our brothers in faith, then we are not of God (1 John 3:10). Such people cannot receive answers to their prayers. They cannot receive salvation much less experience the work of God.

John 8:44 says, *"You are of your father the devil, and you want to do the desires of your father. He was a murderer from the beginning, and does not stand in the truth because there is no truth in him. Whenever he speaks a lie, he speaks from his own nature, for he is a liar and the father of lies."*

Because of Adam's disobedience, all mankind is born as children of the enemy devil, who is the ruler of darkness. Only those who receive forgiveness by believing in Jesus Christ are born anew as God's children. However, if you claim to believe in Jesus Christ and yet your heart continues to be full of sins and evil, then you cannot be called a true child of God.

If we want to become children of God and receive salvation, we need to quickly repent of all our works of the flesh and things of the flesh and bear appropriate fruit of repentance by acting according to the desires of the Holy Spirit.

Do not suppose Abraham is your father

After proclaiming to the Pharisees and Sadducees to bear the fruit in keeping with repentance, John the Baptist went on to say, *"And do not suppose that you can say to yourselves, 'We have Abraham for our father'; for I say to you that from these stones God is able to raise up children to Abraham'"* (Matthew 3:9).

What is the spiritual meaning behind this verse? A descendant of Abraham should resemble Abraham. But unlike Abraham, the father of faith and a man of righteousness, the Pharisees and Sadducees were full of lawlessness and unrighteousness in their hearts. While committing evil acts and obeying the devil, they considered themselves to be children of God. This is why John rebuked them by comparing them to Abraham. God sees the center of man's heart, and not outward appearances (1 Samuel 16:7).

Romans 9:6-8 reads, *"But it is not as though the word of God has failed. For they are not all Israel who are descended from Israel; nor are they all children because they are Abraham's descendants, but: 'THROUGH ISAAC YOUR DESCENDANTS WILL BE NAMED.' That is, it is not the children of the flesh who are children of God, but the children of the promise who are regarded as descendants."*

Father Abraham had many sons; however, only the descendants of Isaac became Abraham's true descendants – the descendants of the promise. The Pharisees and Sadducees were Israelites by blood, but unlike Abraham, they did not keep God's Word. So spiritually speaking, they could not be acknowledged as true children of Abraham.

In the same way, just because someone accepts Jesus Christ and attends a church does not mean they automatically become children of God. A child of God refers to a person who received salvation through faith. Furthermore, having faith doesn't just mean *hearing* God's Word. It is putting it into action. If, with our lips we profess to be His child, and yet our hearts are full of unrighteousness that God detests, we cannot call ourselves children of God.

If God had wanted children who acted out of evil, like the Pharisees and the Sadducees, He would have chosen lifeless stones that roll around on the ground to be His children. But that was not God's will.

God wanted to have true children with whom He could share His love. He wanted children like Abraham, who loved God and obeyed His words completely and who acted out of love and goodness all the time. This is because people who do not cast out evil from their hearts cannot bring true joy to God. If we live like the Pharisees and Sadducees, following the devil's will instead of God's will, then God had no need to put so much effort into making man and cultivating him. He might as well have taken stones and turn them into Abraham's descendants!

"Every tree that does not bear good fruit is cut down and thrown into the fire"

John the Baptist said to the Pharisees and Sadducees, *"The axe is already laid at the root of the trees; therefore every tree that does not bear good fruit is cut down and thrown into the fire"* (Matthew 3:10). What John means here is, because God's Word has been declared, everyone will be judged according to his actions. Therefore any tree that does not bear good fruit—

like the Pharisees and Sadducees—will be thrown into the fire of Hell.

In Matthew 7:17-21, Jesus said, *"So every good tree bears good fruit, but the bad tree bears bad fruit. A good tree cannot produce bad fruit, nor can a bad tree produce good fruit. Every tree that does not bear good fruit is cut down and thrown into the fire. So then, you will know them by their fruits. Not everyone who says to Me, 'Lord, Lord,' will enter the kingdom of heaven, but he who does the will of My Father who is in heaven will enter."*

Jesus also said in John 15:5-6, *"I am the vine, you are the branches; he who abides in Me and I in him, he bears much fruit, for apart from Me you can do nothing. If anyone does not abide in Me, he is thrown away as a branch and dries up; and they gather them, and cast them into the fire and they are burned."* This means that children of God who act according to His will and bear beautiful fruits will enter into Heaven, but those people who do not do this are children of the devil and will be thrown into the fire of Hell.

When the Bible talks about Hell, often the word 'fire' is used. Revelations 21:8 says, *"But for the cowardly and unbelieving and abominable and murderers and immoral persons and sorcerers and idolaters and all liars, their part will be in the lake that burns with fire and brimstone, which is the second death."* The first death is when a person's physical life ends, and the second death is when the soul, or the master of the person, receives judgment and falls into the eternal fire of Hell which never dies.

Hell is made up of the lake of fire and lake of burning sulfur, or 'brimstone'. Those people who do not believe in God, and those who claim to believe in Him but practice unrighteousness and do not bear fruits of repentance have nothing to do with God; therefore they will go into the lake of fire in Hell. Now those people who did something that is so evil that it is humanly unthinkable, or opposed God in a serious way, or acted as a false prophet and caused many people to go to Hell will go into the lake of burning sulfur, which is seven times hotter than the lake of fire (Revelations 19:20).

Some argue that once you receive the Holy Spirit and your name is recorded in the Book of Life, you will be saved no matter what. However, that is not true. Revelations 3:1 reads, *"I know your deeds, that you have a name that you are alive, but you are dead."* Revelations 3:5 says, *"He who overcomes will thus be clothed in white garments; and I will not erase his name from the book of life, and I will confess his name before My Father and before His angels."* "You have a name that you are alive" refers to those who accepted Jesus Christ and had their name recorded in the Book of Life. However, this passage shows that nevertheless, if one sins and goes to the way of death, his name can be erased from the book.

In Exodus 32:32-33, we see the scene where God is angry with the Israelites and is on the verge of destroying them because of their idol worshipping. At this time, Moses interceded on behalf of the sons of Israel by asking God to forgive them – even if it means erasing his own name from the Book of Life. And at that, God said, *"Whoever has sinned against Me, I will blot him out of My book"* (Exodus 32:33). This means even if your name was recorded in the book, it can be erased if you fall away from God.

There are actually many places throughout the Bible that talk about separating the wheat and the chaff among believers. Matthew 3:12 says, *"His winnowing fork is in His hand, and He will thoroughly clear His threshing floor; and He will gather His wheat into the barn, but He will burn up the chaff with unquenchable fire."* Also Matthew 13:49-50 says, *"So it will be at the end of the age; the angels will come forth and take out the wicked from among the righteous, and will throw them into the furnace of fire; in that place there will be weeping and gnashing of teeth."*

Here, "the righteous" refers to believers, and "the wicked among the righteous" refers to those who claim to be believers but just like the chaff, have dead faith, that is, faith without action. These people will be thrown into the fire of Hell.

The fruit in keeping with repentance

John the Baptist urged people not only to repent, but at the same time to bear fruit in keeping with repentance. Then what are the fruits in keeping with repentance? They are the fruits of light, fruits of the Holy Spirit, and fruits of love, which are the beautiful fruits of the truth.

We can read about this in Galatians 5:22-23, *"But the fruit of the Spirit is love, joy, peace, patience, kindness, goodness, faithfulness, gentleness, self-control; against such things there is no law."* And Ephesians 5:9 says, *"For the fruit of the*

Light consists in all goodness and righteousness and truth..." Among all these, let's take a look at the nine fruits of the Holy Spirit, which is an excellent representation of these 'good fruits'.

The first fruit is love. 1 Corinthians chapter 13 tells us what true love is saying that *'it [love] is patient, kind, is not jealous, it does not brag, it is not arrogant, it does not act unbecomingly, etc.'* (vv. 4-5). In other words, true love is spiritual love. Furthermore, this type of love is sacrificial love with which one could even give his life for God's kingdom and His righteousness. One can obtain this kind of love as much as he casts out sin, evil, and lawlessness and become sanctified.

The second fruit is joy. People who have the fruit of joy can be joyful not only when things go well, but they have joy in all circumstances and situations. They are always joyful in the midst of the hope of Heaven. Therefore they do not worry; and no matter what problems come their way, they pray with faith, thereby receiving answers to their prayers. Because they believe that the almighty God is their Father, they can rejoice always, pray continually, and give thanks in all circumstances.

Peace is the third fruit. A person with this fruit has a heart that clashes with no one. Because such people do not have hatred, inclination toward fighting or quarrelling, self-centeredness, or selfishness, they can put others first, sacrifice for them, serve them, and treat them with kindness. As a result, they can achieve peace at all times.

The fourth fruit is patience. Bearing this fruit means being patient in the truth through understanding and forgiving. This does not mean "looking" patient just by subduing the anger that is boiling inside. It means casting out evils such as anger and rage, and filling up with goodness and truth instead. It is being able to understand all kinds of people and embracing them. And, because a person that bears this fruit has no negative emotions, there is no need for words like "forgiving" and "being patient" at all. Not only does this fruit pertain to relationships with people, but it also means being patient with oneself while casting out the evil in his heart and waiting patiently until the prayers and petitions lifted up to God are answered.

The fifth fruit, kindness, is to be understanding when something or someone is impossible to understand. This kindness is also forgiving when it is impossible to forgive. If you have self-centered thoughts or if you feel you are right all the time, you cannot bear the fruit of mercy. Only when you forsake yourself, embrace all things with a broad heart, and look after other people with love, can you truly understand and forgive.

The sixth fruit is goodness. It is imitating the heart of Christ: a heart that never argues or becomes ostentatious; not breaking off a battered reed, nor putting out a smoldering wick. This is a true heart which, having cast out all sins, always seeks goodness in the Holy Spirit.

The seventh fruit is faithfulness. It is being faithful to the point of death – when it comes to fighting against sin and casting it out, in order to achieve truth in your heart. It is also being loyal and faithful when it comes to fulfilling your duties in the church, home, work, or whatever duties you have. It is being faithful in "all God's household".

The eighth fruit is gentleness. Having the fruit of gentleness means having a heart that is soft like cotton, which enables one to embrace all types of people. If you achieve a gentle heart, no matter who comes and tries to offend you, you will not be offended, or hurt. Just like when someone throws a piece of rock into a big piece of cotton, and it just embraces the rock and covers it up, if you bear the fruit of gentleness, you can embrace and be a shade for many people who come to you seeking a place to rest.

Lastly, if you bear the fruit of self-control, you can enjoy stability in all areas of your life. And in a life with order, you can bear all the right kinds of fruit in the proper time. Hence, you can enjoy a beautiful and blessed life.

Because God wants us to have beautiful hearts like these, He said in Matthew 5:14, *"You are the light of the world,"* and in verse 16, *"…Let your light shine before men in such a way that they may see your good works, and glorify your Father who is in heaven."* If we can bear the fruits of the Light which are in line with repentance by truly being in the Light, then all goodness and righteousness and truth will overflow in our lives (Ephesians 5:9).

People who bore the fruits in keeping with repentance

When we repent of our sins and bear the fruit in keeping with repentance, then God acknowledges this as faith and blesses us by answering our prayers. God provides mercy when we repent from the depths of our hearts.

During his times of tribulation, Job discovered the evil in his heart and repented in dust and ashes. At that time, God healed all the sore boils on his body and blessed him with double the wealth he had previously. He also blessed him with children even more beautiful than those he had before (Job chapter 42). When Jonah repented while trapped in the stomach of the great fish, God saved him. The people of Nineveh fasted and repented after receiving the warning about God's wrath being upon them because of their sins, and God forgave them (Jonah chapters 2-3). Hezekiah, the 13th king of the southern kingdom of Judah, was told by God, *"You shall die and not live."* However, when he cried out in repentance, God extended his life by 15 years (2 Kings chapter 20).

It is in this way that even though someone commits an evil deed, if he or she repents from the center of his or her heart, and truly turns away from the sin, God receives that repentance. God saves His people, as it is written in Psalm 103:12, *"As far as the east is from the west, so far has He removed our transgressions from us."*

In 2 Kings chapter 4, we see one prominent woman of Shunem who faithfully served the prophet Elisha with her hospitality. Even though she did not ask, she received a son, whom she had long desired. She did not serve to receive a blessing, but she served Elisha because she loved and cared for God's servant. God was pleased with her good deed and blessed her with the blessing of conception.

Also, in Acts chapter 9, we see Tabitha, a disciple who was abounding with deeds of kindness and charity. When she became ill and died, God used Peter to bring her back to life. To those loving children that bear beautiful fruits, God wants so much to answer their prayers, and give them His grace and blessings.

Therefore we must clearly know God's will, and bear the fruits in keeping with repentance. We should then imitate the heart of our Lord and practice righteousness. Reflecting yourself upon the Word of God, if any part of your life is not in accordance with God's Word, I pray that you will turn back to Him, thereby bearing fruits of the Holy Spirit, fruits of Light, and fruits of love, so that you can receive the answers to all of your prayers.

Glossary

The difference between sin and evil

"Sin" is any deed that is not in accordance with faith. It is not doing the right thing while knowing it is the right thing to do. In a wider scope, everything that has nothing to do with faith is a sin; therefore not believing in Jesus Christ is the greatest sin.

"Evil" is anything that is unacceptable when reflected upon God's Word, that is, everything contrary to the truth. It is the sinful natures that reside in the heart. Accordingly, sin is a specific, outwardly expression, or visible form of the evil inside of one's heart. Evil is invisible in nature; therefore sin is established as a result of the evil in one's heart.

What is goodness?

In the dictionary, goodness is "the state or quality of being good, moral excellence, virtue". However, depending on each person's conscience, the standard of goodness can be different. Therefore the absolute standard for goodness must be found in the Word of God who is goodness itself. Therefore, goodness is truth, namely God's Word. It is His very will and thought.

Chapter 5

"Abhor What is Evil; Cling to What is Good."

*"Let love be without hypocrisy.
Abhor what is evil;
cling to what is good."*
(Romans 12:9)

In this day and age we can see evil existing in the relationships between parents and their children, between spouses, between brothers and sisters and between neighbors. People sue each other over their inheritance, and in some cases, people betray one another just for their own benefit. This not only causes others to frown upon them; but it also brings great suffering upon themselves. This is why God said, *"Abstain from every form of evil"* (1 Thessalonians 5:22).

The world calls a person 'good' when he or she is morally upright and conscientious. However, there are many cases when even a person's 'good' morals and conscience are not so good when reflected against God's Word. Furthermore, there are times when they actually contradict the very will of God. One truth we must remember here is that God's Word—and His Word only—is the absolute standard for 'goodness'. Therefore, everything and anything that is not fully in accordance with God's Word is evil.

Then how are sin and evil different? These two things seem to be alike, but they are different. For instance, if we use a tree as an illustration, evil is like the roots that are under the ground and invisible, while sin is like the visible parts of the tree, which are branches, leaves, and fruits. Just as a tree can live because it has its roots, a person sins because of the evil inside of him. Evil is one of the natures within a person's heart, and it encompasses all the traits and conditions that are contradictory to God. When this evil takes on an expressed form as thought or action then it is called "sin".

How evil is displayed as sin

Luke 6:45 says, *"The good man out of the good treasure of his heart brings forth what is good; and the evil man out of the evil treasure brings forth what is evil; for his mouth speaks from that which fills his heart."* If 'hate' exists in the heart, it comes out in the form of 'sarcastic remarks', 'harsh words', or other specific sins like these. In order to see how evil that is inside the heart comes out in the form of sin, let us take a closer look at David and Judas Iscariot.

One night, as King David was walking along the rooftop of his palace, he saw a woman taking a bath and became tempted. He called for her and committed adultery with her. That woman was Bathsheba, and at that time, her husband, Uriah, was not there because he had gone to war. When David found out Bathsheba was pregnant, he plotted to have Uriah killed at the battlefront and took Bathsheba as his wife.

Of course David only appointed Uriah to spearhead the war—he didn't actually kill him—and at that time, as king, David had every power and authority to have as many wives as he wanted. However, in David's heart, he had clear intent for Uriah to be killed. In this way, if you have evil in some area of your heart, you can sin at any time.

As a consequence of that sin, the son that David had with Bathsheba died; and his other son, Absalom, ended up betraying him and committing treason against him. As a result, David had to flee, and Absalom committed the detestable act of sleeping with his father's concubines in front of his people in broad daylight. Due to this event, many people in the kingdom died, including Absalom. The sin of adultery and murder brought about great tribulation for David and his people.

Judas Iscariot, one of Jesus' twelve disciples, is a prime example of a betrayer. During the 3 years that he spent with Jesus, he saw all kinds of miracles that could only occur by God's power. He took care of the money bag among the disciples, and he had trouble casting out greed from his heart, and from time to time, he took money from the bag and used it according to his own needs. Ultimately, his greed caused him to betray his teacher, and his own guilt caused him to hang himself.

So if there is evil in your heart, you never know in what shape or form that evil will come out. Even if that is a small form of evil, if it grows, Satan can work through it to drive you into sin where you yourself cannot avoid it. You may end up betraying another person, or even God. This kind of evil brings pain and suffering to you and people around you. This is the reason why you must hate what is evil and cast away even the smallest form of evil. If you hate what is evil, you will naturally distance yourself from that evil, you won't think about it, and you won't carry it out. You will only do good. This is why God said to hate what is evil.

The reason why disease, tests, trials and tribulations come upon us is because we committed works of the flesh by allowing the evil inside of our hearts to be expressed outwardly as sin. If we do not control our hearts and commit works of the flesh, we are no different from animals in God's eyes. If this is the case, there will be God's wrath, and He chastises us, so we can be like men again, and not like animals.

To cast out evil and become a person of goodness

Trials and tribulations do not come just because of thoughts of untruth or things of the flesh that exist in the heart. But the thoughts can develop into works of the flesh (sinful acts) at any time, and thus we must get rid of the things of the flesh.

Above all, if one does not believe in God even after seeing miracles manifested by Him, it is the evil among all evils. In Matthew 11:20-24, Jesus denounced the cities in which most of His miracles were done, because they did not repent. To Chorazin and Bethsaida, Jesus said, *"Woe to you,"* and He warned, *"It will be more bearable for Tyre and Sidon on the day of judgment than for you."* And to Capernaum He said, *"It will be more bearable for Sodom on the day of judgment than for you."*

Tyre and Sidon refer to two gentile cities. Bethsaida and

Chorazin are Israeli cities north of the Sea of Galilee. Bethsaida is also the hometown of three of the disciples: Peter, Andrew, and Phillip. This is where Jesus opened the eyes of a blind man, and where He performed the great miracle of the two fish and five loaves with which He fed 5,000 men. Since they witnessed miracles that gave them more than enough evidence to believe in Jesus, they should have followed, repented, and cast out evil from their hearts according to His teachings. But, they did not do this. This is why they were chastised.

The same goes for us today. If a person witnesses signs and wonders being performed by a person of God and he or she still does not believe in God, but instead judges and condemns the situation or the person of God, then the person is demonstrating the evidence that there is evil inside of his heart. Then why can't the people believe? It's because they have to subdue and cast out things of the flesh, but they don't do this. Instead they commit works of the flesh and commit sins. The more they commit sins, the more callous and hardened their hearts become. Their consciences become desensitized and ultimately seared as with a hot iron.

Even though God demonstrates miracles for them to see, people like this are not able to gain understanding and believe. Since there is no understanding, they cannot repent, and because they do not repent, they cannot accept Jesus Christ. This is like a person who steals. At first, the person is afraid of stealing even one small object; but after repeating the act a couple of times, he doesn't even feel a pang of conscience after stealing a big object, because his heart has become hardened through the process.

If we love God, it is only right that we abhor evil and cling to what is good. In order to do this, we need to first stop committing all works of the flesh and then cast out all the things of the flesh from our hearts as well.

And when we are in the process of casting out sin and evil, we can build a relationship with God and receive His love (1 John 1:7, 3:9). Our faces will always reflect overflowing joy and thanksgiving, we can receive healing from any kind of illness, and we can receive solutions to any problems we may have in our families, work, business, etc.

An evil and adulterous generation that craves a sign

In Matthew 12:38-39, we see some of the scribes and Pharisees demanding Jesus to show them a sign. Jesus then told them that an evil and adulterous generation craves to see a sign. For example, there are people who say, "If you show me God, I will believe," or "If you bring a dead person back to life I will believe." These people are not saying this with an innocent heart that is genuinely seeking to believe. They are saying this out of doubt.

So this tendency not to believe in the truth, or the inclination to ostracize or doubt someone that is better than themselves, or the desire to reject anything that doesn't agree with their own thinking or views, all come from a spiritually adulterous nature. While refusing to believe, the people that demanded to see a sign conspired and strained to fish out some kind of flaw in Jesus—in order to proscribe and condemn Him.

The more self-righteousness, arrogance, and selfishness people have, the more adulterous that generation becomes. As a civilization becomes more advanced like today, more people demand to see signs. However, there are so many people who see signs and still do not believe! No wonder this type of generation is reprimanded for being an evil and adulterous generation!

If you hate evil, you will not practice evil. If feces get on your body, you will wash it off. Sin and evil, which decays the soul and drags it to the way of death, is even filthier, smellier, and uglier than feces. We cannot compare the filthiness of sins to that of feces.

Then exactly what types of evil should we hate? In Matthew chapter 23, Jesus reprimands the scribes and Pharisees by saying, *"Woe to you…"* He uses the phrase "Woe to you," signifying that they will not receive salvation. And we will divide the reasons into seven categories and study them in more detail.

The forms of evil we should abhor

1. Closing the door of Heaven so other people cannot enter

In Matthew 23:13, Jesus says, *"But woe to you, scribes and Pharisees, hypocrites, because you shut off the kingdom of heaven from people; for you do not enter in yourselves, nor do you allow those who are entering to go in."*

The scribes and Pharisees knew and recorded God's words and acted like they were keeping God's words. But their hearts were hardened, and they did God's work superficially—hence, they were reprimanded. Though they had all the formalities of holiness, their hearts were teeming with lawlessness and evil.

When they saw Jesus performing miracles that are humanly impossible, instead of recognizing who He was and rejoicing, they conjured up all kinds of plots to oppose Him. They even spearheaded His death.

This is true for people in this age as well. People who claim to believe in Jesus Christ and yet do not live a model life fall into this category. If you make someone say, "I do not want to believe in Jesus because of people like you," then you are the person shutting off the kingdom of heaven from people. Not only are you not entering into Heaven; but you are also keeping others from entering as well.

People who claim to believe in God, but continue to compromise with the world are also those that Jesus reprimanded. If in the order of the church, a person with a church title that is in a position of teaching shows hatred toward another person, becomes angry, or acts out of disobedience, how can a new Christian look at this person and trust him, let alone respect him? They will more than likely become disappointed and maybe even lose their faith. If, among non-believers there are those whose wives or husbands are trying to grow in their faith, and they either persecute them or make them act out of evil and partake in sin, they will also receive a "Woe to you" reprimanding.

2. When one becomes a proselyte, making him twice as much as a son of Hell as yourself

In Matthew 23:15, Jesus says, *"Woe to you, scribes and Pharisees, hypocrites, because you travel around on sea and land to make one proselyte; and when he becomes one, you make him twice as much a son of hell as yourselves."*

There is an old saying that a daughter-in-law who received a hard time from her mother-in-law will give a harder time to her daughter-in-law. What a person sees and experiences becomes embedded in his memory, and subconsciously, he acts according to what he experienced. This is why what you learn and from whom you learn is very important. If you learn the Christian walk from people like the scribes and Pharisees, then like the blind leading another blind, you will fall into evil together with them.

For example, if a leader is always judging and condemning others, gossiping and speaking negatively, the believers learning from him will also become tainted by his actions, and together they will go to the way of death. In society, children that grow up in homes where their parents are constantly fighting and hating one another have a higher chance of being led astray than those children that grow up in peaceful homes.

Therefore, parents, teachers, and other leaders need to be better examples, above all others. If the words and actions of these kinds of people are not exemplary, they could really cause others to stumble. Even in the church, there are cases where a servant or a leader is not a good model, and they end up obstructing the revival or growth of their small group, department, or organization. We must realize that if this is what we are doing, we are causing not only ourselves, but others as well, to become sons of Hell.

3. Delivering the will of God in a wrong way due to greed and falsehood

In Matthew 23:16-22, Jesus says, *"Woe to you, blind guides, who say, 'Whoever swears by the temple, that is nothing; but whoever swears by the gold of the temple is obligated.' You fools and blind men! Which is more important, the gold or the temple that sanctified the gold? And, 'Whoever swears by the altar, that is nothing, but whoever swears by the offering on it, he is obligated.' You blind men, which is more important, the offering, or the altar that sanctifies the offering? Therefore, whoever swears by the altar, swears both by the altar and by everything on it. And whoever swears by the temple, swears both by the temple and by Him who dwells within it. And whoever swears by heaven, swears both by the throne of God and by Him who sits upon it."*

This message is a reprimand against those who falsely teach God's will out of greed, deceit, and selfishness in their hearts. If someone makes a vow or promise to God, the teachers should teach him to keep that promise, but the teachers were teaching the people to put that aside and just keep the promises they made regarding money, or material possessions. If a minister neglects teaching people to live in the truth and only emphasizes on offerings, then he is being a leader that has gone blind.

Before anything else, a leader must teach the people to repent of their sins, cultivate the righteousness of God, and hence enter into the kingdom of heaven. Making an oath by the temple, Jesus Christ, the altar, and the Heavenly Throne is all the same, therefore one must be sure to keep that oath.

4. Neglecting the weightier provisions of the Law

In Matthew 23:23-24, Jesus says, *"Woe to you, scribes and*

Pharisees, hypocrites! For you tithe mint and dill and cummin, and have neglected the weightier provisions of the law: justice and mercy and faithfulness; but these are the things you should have done without neglecting the others. You blind guides, who strain out a gnat and swallow a camel!"

A person who truly believes in God will give whole tithes. If we give whole tithes, we receive blessings; but if we do not, we are robbing God (Malachi 3:8-10). Yes, the scribes and Pharisees gave their tithes; but Jesus scorned them for neglecting justice, mercy, and faithfulness. Then what does it mean to neglect justice, mercy, and faithfulness?

'Justice' signifies casting off sin, living according to God's Word, and obeying Him with faith. Being 'obedient', according to worldly standards, is to obey and do something that you are able to do. However, in the truth, being 'obedient' is being able to obey and do the things that seem absolutely impossible to do so.

In the Bible, the prophets that were acknowledged by God obeyed His words with faith. They parted the Red Sea, destroyed the wall of Jericho, and stopped the flow of the Jordan River. If they had input their human thoughts into the situation, these things could never have happened. But with faith, they obeyed God and made them possible.

'Mercy' is to fulfill your whole duty as man in all aspects of your life. There are basic morals and ethics in this world that people can abide by to keep themselves human. However, these standards are not perfect. Even if a person appears cultured and refined on the outside, if he has evil inside of him, we cannot say he is truly refined. In order for us to truly live a life that is worthy, we need to do the whole duty of men, which is obeying God's commands (Ecclesiastes 12:13).

Also, 'faithfulness' is to partake in God's divine nature through faith (2 Peter 1:4). God's purpose in creating the heavens and the earth, all things in them, and the mankind, is to gain true children that reflect His heart. God told us to be true, as He is true, and to be perfect, as He is perfect. We should not have the mere appearance of holiness. Only by casting out evil from our hearts and completely abiding by His commandments can we truly partake in God's divine nature.

However, the scribes and Pharisees of Jesus' time neglected justice, mercy, and faithfulness, and only focused on offerings and sacrifices. God is much more pleased with a repenting heart, rather than sacrifices offered with untruthful hearts (Psalm 51:16-17). However, they were teaching something that was not tuned with God's will. A person who is in a position of teaching should first point out the people's sins, help them bear fruits in keeping with repentance, and lead them to have peace with God. After that, they should teach about giving tithes, the formalities of worship, prayer, etc., until they reach complete salvation.

5. Keeping the outside clean while leaving the inside full of robbery and self-indulgence

In Matthew 23:25-26, Jesus said, *"Woe to you, scribes and Pharisees, hypocrites! For you clean the outside of the cup and of the dish, but inside they are full of robbery and self-indulgence. You blind Pharisee, first clean the inside of the cup and of the dish, so that the outside of it may become clean also."*

When you look at a clear glass made of crystal, it is very clean and beautiful. However, depending on what you put inside the cup, it could shine more beautifully, or it could become tainted. If it is filled with filthy water, it can only become a filthy cup. In the same way, even if someone appears to be a person of God on the outside, if his heart is full of evil, God, who sees the heart, will see all the filth inside, and consider him tainted.

In people's relationships too, no matter how clean, well-dressed, and well-cultured a person may seem on the outside, if we discover that they are full of hate, envy, jealousy, and all kinds of evil, we feel the uncleanliness and shame. Then how would God, who is righteousness and truth itself, feel, when He sees people like these? Therefore we must reflect ourselves on the Word of God and repent of all debauchery and greed, and strive to achieve a clean heart. If we act according to God's Word and continue to cast out sins, our hearts will become clean, so our outward appearance will naturally become clean and holy.

6. Being like whitewashed tombs

In Matthew 23:27-28, Jesus says, *"Woe to you, scribes and Pharisees, hypocrites! For you are like whitewashed tombs which on the outside appear beautiful, but inside they are full of dead men's bones and all uncleanness. So you, too, outwardly appear righteous to men, but inwardly you are full of hypocrisy and lawlessness."*

No matter how much money you spend on trying to beautify a tomb, ultimately, what is inside of it? A decaying corpse that will soon turn into a handful of dust! Therefore a whitewashed tomb symbolizes the hypocrites who are only well-groomed on the outside. They look good, gentle, and wholesome on the outside, advising and scolding others, while on the inside they are actually full of hate, envy, jealousy, adultery, etc.

If we confess to believe in God and we keep the hatred in our hearts as we condemn others, then we are seeing the speck in other people's eyes and not seeing the plank in our own eyes. This is what is considered as hypocrisy. This can be applied to non-believers as well. Having a heart that inclines toward betraying one's husband or wife, neglecting one's children, or not honoring one's parents, while mocking the truth and criticizing others is also an act of hypocrisy.

7. Considering yourself righteous

In Matthew 23:29-33, Jesus says, *"Woe to you, scribes and Pharisees, hypocrites! For you build the tombs of the prophets and adorn the monuments of the righteous, and say, 'If we had been living in the days of our fathers, we would not have been partners with them in shedding the blood of the prophets.' So you testify against yourselves, that you are sons of those who murdered the prophets. Fill up, then, the measure of the guilt of your fathers. You serpents, you brood of vipers, how will you escape the sentence of hell?"*

The hypocritical scribes and Pharisees built the tombs of the prophets and adorned the monuments of the righteous and said, *"If we had been living in the days of our fathers, we would not have been partners with them in shedding the blood of the prophets."* However, this confession is not true. Not only did these scribes and Pharisees not recognize Jesus, who came as the Savior, but they rejected Him, and ultimately nailed Him to the cross and killed Him. How can they call themselves more righteous than their ancestors?

Jesus scorned these hypocritical leaders by saying, *"Fill up, then, the measure of the guilt of your fathers."* When a person sins, if he has even a hint of conscience, he will feel guilty and stop sinning. But there are also those people who don't turn away from their evil actions to the bitter end. This is what Jesus meant when He said "fill up". They became children of the devil, the brood of vipers, and acted with even more evil.

Likewise, if a person hears the truth and feels a pang of conscience, and yet considers himself righteous and refuses to repent, then he is no different from a person who fills up the measure of guit his ancestor committed. Jesus said if these people do not repent and bear the fruit keeping with repentance, then they cannot escape the sentence of Hell.

Therefore, we must reflect ourselves upon the chastisement Jesus gave to the scribes and Pharisees and see if there is anything that pertains to us, and quickly cast those things out. I hope you, the reader, will be a righteous person who hates evil and clings to what is good, thereby giving all glory to God and enjoying a blessed life—as much as your heart desires!

Glossary and further clarification

What is 'human cultivation'?

'Cultivation' is the process where a farmer sows a seed, takes care of it, and bears fruit by it. In order to gain true children of His, God planted Adam and Eve here in this world as the first fruits. After the fall of Adam, mankind became sinners, and after receiving Jesus Christ and with the help of the Holy Spirit, they were able to recover the true image of God that were once in them. So the whole process of God creating man and overseeing the entire history of mankind up to the last judgment is called 'human cultivation'.

The difference between the 'body', the 'flesh', and the 'things of the flesh'

Normally, when we refer to the human body, we use the terms 'body' and 'flesh' interchangeably. However, in the Bible, each of these words has a specific spiritual meaning. There are times when 'flesh' is used simply to signify the human body, but spiritually, it refers to those things that decay, change, are unwholesome and dirty.

The first person, Adam, was a living spirit, and he had no sin whatsoever. However, after being tempted through Satan to eat the fruit of the knowledge of good and evil, he had to experience death, for the wages of sin is death (Genesis 2:17; Romans 6:23). God planted the knowledge of life, the truth, inside of man at creation. The shape or form of man without this truth, which leaked out after Adam sinned, is referred to as the 'body'. And the sinful nature combined within this body is referred to as 'the flesh'. This flesh does not have a visible form, but it is a sinful nature which can be provoked to come out at any time.

The soil of man's heart

The Bible categorizes man's heart into different types of soil: the roadside, the rocky soil, the thorny soil, and the good soil (Mark chapter 4).

The roadside signifies a hard and calloused heart. Even if a seed of God's Word is planted into this type of heart, the seed cannot sprout, and it cannot bear fruit; therefore the person cannot receive salvation.

The rocky soil signifies a person who understands God's Word with their head, but he cannot believe with his heart. While listening to the Word, he may make a commitment to apply what he learned, but when hardship comes, he cannot keep his faith.

The thorny soil refers to the heart of a person who listens, understands, and applies the Word of God to their lives, but he cannot overcome the temptations of this world. He is enticed by the worries of this world, greed, and fleshly desires, so trials and tribulations follow, and he cannot grow spiritually.

The good soil signifies a person's heart where, when God's Word falls into it, the Word bears fruit 30, 60, 100 times, and God's blessings and answers always follow.

The role of Satan and the devil

Satan is a being that has the power of darkness that causes people to do evil things. It has no specific form. It constantly spreads its dark heart, thoughts, and its power to do evil into the air like a radiowave. And when the untruth inside of a man's heart catches its frequency, it uses the man's thoughts to pour its dark powers into him. This is what we call "receiving the work of Satan", or "listening to the voice of Satan".

The devil is a part of the angels that fell along with Lucifer. They are dressed in black, and it has facial features and hands and feet like a person or an angel. It takes orders from Satan and maintains and gives commands to numerous demons to bring illnesses to people and makes them fall into sin and evil.

The character of vessel and the character of heart

People are referred to as 'vessels'. The character of vessel of a person depends on how well he listens to the Word of God and inscribes it in his heart, and how well he carries it out as action with faith. The character of vessel has to do with the type of material it is made from. If a person has a good character of vessel, he can become sanctified very quickly, and he can exhibit spiritual powers in a wider scope. In order to cultivate a good character of vessel, one should listen to the Word properly and inscribe it in the center of his heart. How diligently one carries out what he learned determines one's character of vessel.

The character of the heart depends on how widely the heart is used, and the size of the vessel. There are the cases of 1) going beyond one's capacity, 2) just filling one's capacity, 3) grudgingly filling the barely minimum capacity, and 4) the case where it is better off for one not to have begun his work in the first place because of all the evil he commits. If the character of one's heart is small and lacking, he or she needs to work on transforming it into a wider, bigger heart.

Righteousness in God's sight

The first level of righteousness is the casting out of sins. At this level the person is justified by accepting Jesus Christ and receiving the Holy Spirit. Then, he discovers his sins and diligently prays to cast those sins away. God is pleased with this act, and answers the person's prayers and blesses him.

The second level of righteousness is keeping the Word. After one casts out sins, he can be filled with God's Word in him, and he is able to abide by it. For example, if he heard a message about not hating anyone, he casts out hate and strives to love everyone. It is in this way that he obeys God's Word. At this time, he receives the blessing of being healthy at all times, and every prayer he lifts up is answered.

The third level of righteousness is pleasing God. At this level not only does one cast out sin, but he also acts according to God's will at all times. And he dedicates his life to fulfill his calling. If a person reaches this level, God answers even the smallest wishes he simply conceives in his heart.

Part 2
Concerning Righteousness...

"... and concerning righteousness,
because I go to the Father and you no longer see Me;"
(John 16:10)

"Then he believed in the LORD; and He reckoned it to him as righteousness." (Genesis 15:6)

"For I say to you that unless your righteousness surpasses that of the scribes and Pharisees, you will not enter the kingdom of heaven." (Matthew 5:20)

"But now apart from the Law the righteousness of God has been manifested, being witnessed by the Law and the Prophets, even the righteousness of God through faith in Jesus Christ for all those who believe; for there is no distinction;" (Romans 3:21-22)

"...having been filled with the fruit of righteousness which comes through Jesus Christ, to the glory and praise of God." (Philippians 1:11)

"... in the future there is laid up for me the crown of righteousness, which the Lord, the righteous Judge, will award to me on that day; and not only to me, but also to all who have loved His appearing." (2 Timothy 4:8)

"... and the Scripture was fulfilled which says, "And Abraham believed God, and it was reckoned to him as righteousness," and he was called the friend of God." (James 2:23)

"By this the children of God and the children of the devil are obvious: anyone who does not practice righteousness is not of God, nor the one who does not love his brother." (1 John 3:10)

Chapter 6

Righteousness That Leads to Life

"So then as through one transgression there resulted condemnation to all men, even so through one act of righteousness there resulted justification of life to all men."
(Romans 5:18)

I met the living God after seven years of being bedridden with sickness. Not only did I receive healing of all my diseases through the fire of the Holy Spirit, but after repenting of my sins, I also received eternal life which would allow me to live in Heaven forever. I was so thankful for God's grace that from the time I began attending church, I stopped drinking, and I stopped serving others with alcoholic drinks.

There once was a time when one of my relatives ridiculed churches. Unable to restrain myself, I said angrily, "Why do you talk bad about God and speak negatively about the church and pastor?" As a baby Christian, I thought my actions were justified. Only later did I realize that my actions were not correct. Righteousness as I saw it took the lead instead of the righteousness as seen in God's eyes. It resulted in quarreling and arguing.

In this kind of situation, what was righteousness in God's sight? It was trying to understand the other person with love. If you just consider the fact that they are acting the way they do because they do not know the Lord and God, then there's no reason to become upset with them. True righteousness is praying for them with love and seeking a wise way to evangelize them and lead them to become a child of God.

Righteousness in God's sight

Exodus 16:26 says, *"If you will give earnest heed to the voice of the LORD your God, and do what is right in His sight..."* This verse tells us the fact that righteousness in man's sight and righteousness in God's sight is clearly different.

In our world, taking revenge is often considered acting righteously. However, God tells us that loving all people and loving even our enemies, is righteousness. Also, the world considers it righteous when someone fights to accomplish what they think is the right thing to do, even at the expense of breaking peace with other people. But God does not consider a person righteous when he breaks peace with others just because of what he thinks is right in his own mind.

Also, in this world, no matter how much evil you have in your heart such as hatred, dissension, envy, jealousy, anger, and selfishness, as long as you do not break the laws of the country and you don't commit any sins in your actions, no one calls you unrighteous. However, even if you don't commit any sins with your actions, if you have evil in your heart, God calls you an unrighteous person. Man's concept of righteousness and unrighteousness varies among different persons, places, and generations. Therefore, in order for us to set a true standard for righteousness and unrighteousness, we must set the standard on God. What God calls righteous is true righteousness.

Now then, what did Jesus do? Romans 5:18 says, *"So then as through one transgression there resulted condemnation to all men, even so through one act of righteousness there resulted justification of life to all men."* Here, the "one transgression" is the sin of Adam, the father of all mankind, and the "one act of righteousness" is the obedience of Jesus, the Son of God. He fulfilled the righteous act of leading many people to life. Let us study in more detail about what this righteousness is, which leads people to life.

The one act of righteousness which saves all of mankind

In Genesis 2:7, we read that God created the first man, Adam, in His image. Then He breathed into his nostrils and made him a living spirit. Just like a new born baby, nothing was registered in him. He was a fresh, new slate. Just as a baby grows and begins compiling and utilizing knowledge through what he sees and hears, he was taught by God about the harmony of the entire universe, the laws of the spiritual realm, and the words of truth.

God taught Adam everything he needed to know in order to

live as the lord of all creation. Now there was only one thing that God forbade. Adam could eat freely from any tree in the Garden of Eden except for the tree of the knowledge of good and evil. God gave him a strong warning that on the day that he ate from it he would surely die (Genesis 2:16-17).

However, after a long time had passed he failed to mark these words and he fell into the temptation of the serpent and ate the forbidden fruit. As a result, his communication with God was severed and as God had said, "You will surely die," Adam's spirit, which was a living spirit, died. Because he did not obey God's Word but listened to the enemy devil's words, he became a child of the devil.

1 John 3:8 says, *"The one who practices sin is of the devil; for the devil has sinned from the beginning."* And John 8:44, *"You are of your father the devil, and you want to do the desires of your father. He was a murderer from the beginning, and does not stand in the truth because there is no truth in him. Whenever he speaks a lie, he speaks from his own nature, for he is a liar and the father of lies."*

If Adam is the one that disobeyed and sinned, then why are his descendants also sinners? A child is bound to take after his parents, especially in their appearance. But his personality and even the way he walks is bound to resemble his parents. This is because a child inherits what is known as his parents' "chi", or "spirit", or "life force", and just as the life force is passed down to the child, the sinful natures of the parents are also passed down (Psalms 51:5). A newborn baby is not taught by anyone to cry and fuss, but he does it on his own. This is because sinful nature is contained in the life-force that was passed down generation after generation all the way from Adam.

In addition to the original sins that man inherits, he also keeps on committing sins on his own, and so his heart becomes more and more tainted with sins. Then he again passes this onto his children. As time passes the world becomes inundated with sin. Then how can man, who has become a child of the devil, restore his relationship with God?

God knew from the beginning that man would sin. Therefore He prepared His providence of salvation and kept it hidden. The salvation of mankind through Jesus Christ was a secret that was hidden since the beginning of time. So Jesus Christ, who was spotless and without blemish, took upon Himself the curse and hung on the cross to open up the way of salvation for the mankind who was destined to die. Through this act of righteousness by Jesus Christ, many people who were once sinners have been freed from death and gained life.

The beginning of righteousness is believing in God

"Righteousness" is to be in accordance with virtue or morality. However "righteousness" according to God is obeying with faith out of reverence for Him, the casting out of sin and keeping His commands (Ecclesiastes 12:13). But above all, the Bible calls the mere act of not believing in God, a sin (John 16:9). Therefore, the simple act of believing in God is an act of righteousness, and it is the first condition one must have in order to become a righteous person.

How can we call a person right or proper if that person

neglects and betrays his parents that gave birth to him? People will point fingers at him and call him a sinner who has no regard for humanity. Likewise, if a person will not believe in the Creator God who created us, if he will not call Him Father, and to top it all off, if he serves the enemy devil—which God hates the most—then this becomes a grave sin.

Therefore, in order to become a righteous person, first and foremost, you must believe in God. Just as Jesus had total faith in God and kept His every word, we too must have faith in Him and keep His words. To have faith in God means to believe in the fact that God is the Lord of all creation who created the entire universe and us, and who is in sole control over the life and death of mankind. It is also believing in the fact that God is self-existing, that He is the first and the last, the beginning and the end. It is to believe that He is the ultimate judge who has prepared Heaven and Hell, and who will judge each person with justice. God sent His only begotten Son, Jesus Christ into this world to open the way of salvation for us. Therefore believing in Jesus Christ and receiving salvation is, in essence, believing in God.

So there is something God requests from all His children who enter through the door of salvation. In this world, citizens of a certain country must abide by the laws of that country. In the same way, if you have become a citizen of Heaven, you should abide by the laws of Heaven that is God's Word, which is the Truth. For example, since Exodus 20:8 says, *"Remember the Sabbath day, to keep it holy,"* you should obey God's law and make it a top priority by keeping the whole Sabbath, and not compromise with the world. We should do this because God considers this kind of faith and obedience as righteousness.

Through Jesus Christ, God enlightened us about the law of righteousness which leads us to life. If we abide by this law we become righteous, we can go to Heaven, and we can receive God's love and blessings.

The righteousness of Jesus Christ which we must emulate

Even Jesus, who is the Son of God, accomplished righteousness by completely abiding by God's laws. Above all else, while He was here on the earth, He never showed even a hint of evil. Because He was conceived by the Holy Spirit, He did not have original sin. And, since He had no thoughts or anything of evil He had no committed sin either.

Most of the time, people show evil actions because they have lawless thoughts. A person who has greed will first think, "How can I gain wealth? How can I take that person's possessions and make it my own?" And then the person will plant this thought in his heart. And when his heart is agitated, he will most likely take evil actions. Because he has greed in his heart, he is tempted by Satan through his thoughts; and when he accepts this temptation, he ends up taking evil actions such as cheating, embezzling, and stealing.

Job 15:35 says, *"They conceive mischief and bring forth iniquity, and their mind prepares deception."* And in Genesis 6:5 it says that before God's judgment of the world through the flood, man's wickedness was great on the earth, and that every intent of the thoughts the heart of man was continually evil. Because the heart is evil, the mind is evil as well. However, if there is no evil in our heart, Satan cannot work through our thoughts to tempt us. Just as it is written that things that proceed from the mouth come from the heart (Matthew 15:18), if the heart is not evil, there is no way evil thoughts or actions can come out from it.

Jesus, who had neither original sin nor self-committed sins, had a heart which was holiness in itself. Therefore all of His actions were always good. Because His heart was righteous, He only had righteous thoughts and He only took righteous actions. In order for us to become righteous people we must protect our thoughts by casting out the evil in our hearts, and then our actions will be wholesome as well.

If we obey and do exactly what the Bible says to "Do, don't do, keep, and cast out", the heart of God, or the truth, will dwell in our hearts so that we do not sin with our thoughts. And our actions will also become wholesome by receiving the guidance and direction of the Holy Spirit. God says 'keep the Sunday holy', so we keep the Sunday holy. He says 'pray, love, and share the gospel', so we pray, love, and share the gospel. He says do not steal or commit adultery, so we do not do these things.

And since He told us to cast out even the forms of evil, we continue to cast out untruths such as jealousy, envy, hate, adultery, deceit, etc. And, if we abide by God's Word, then the untruths in our hearts disappear and only the truth is left. If we pull out the bitter roots of sin from our hearts, sin can no longer enter us through our thoughts. Therefore, whatever we see, we see out of goodness and whatever we might say and do is also said and done out of the goodness coming from our hearts.

Proverbs 4:23 says, *"Watch over your heart with all*

diligence, for from it flow the springs of life." The righteousness that leads to life, or the source of life, comes from protecting the heart. In order for us to obtain life we must keep righteousness, namely the truth, in our heart and abide by it. This is why it is so important to protect one's mind and heart.

But because there is so much evil inside of us, we cannot possibly cast all of them out solely with our own strengths. In addition to our own efforts to cast out sin, we also need the power of the Holy Spirit. This is why we need prayer. When we pray with fiery prayers, God's grace and power comes upon us and we become filled with the Holy Spirit. That's when we can cast out those sins!

James 3:17 says, *"But the wisdom from above is first pure…"* This means that when we cast out the sins of our hearts and focus only on righteousness, then wisdom from above comes upon us. However great the wisdom of the world may be, it could never compare to the wisdom that comes from above. The wisdom of this world comes from man, who is limited and cannot foresee even a second's worth of what is to come. However, the wisdom that comes from above is sent down by the Almighty God so we can even know about the things that are to come in the future and prepare for it.

In Luke 3:40 it says that Jesus 'grew and became strong, increasing in wisdom'. It is recorded that by the time He was at twelve years of age, He was so wise that even the Rabbis who had thorough knowledge of the Law were awed by His wisdom. Because Jesus' mind was only focused on righteousness, He received wisdom from above.

1 Peter 2:22-23 says, *"...who[Jesus] committed no sin, nor was any deceit found in His mouth; and while being reviled, He did not revile in return; while suffering, He uttered no threats..."* Through this verse, we can see Jesus' heart. Also in John 4:34, when the disciples brought food, Jesus said, *"My food is to do the will of Him who sent Me and to accomplish His work."* Because Jesus' heart and mind were only focused on righteousness, all of His actions were always wholesome.

Jesus was not only faithful in doing God's work; He was faithful in "all God's household." Even while dying on the cross, He entrusted Virgin Mary to John, to make sure she was cared for. So, Jesus fully completed His worldly duty as a person, while preaching the gospel of the kingdom of heaven and healing the sick with God's power. He ultimately completed His mission for coming into this world by taking up the cross to take care of mankind's sins and weaknesses. That is how He became the Savior of mankind, the King of kings and the Lord of lords.

The way of becoming a righteous person

Then as children of God, what should we do? We need to become righteous people by keeping God's laws through our actions. Since Jesus became a supreme model for all of us by keeping and practicing all of God's laws, we need to do the same by following His example.

Practicing God's laws means to keep His commandments and be without blemish regarding His statutes. The Ten Commandments would be the prime example of God's commandments. The Commandments can be thought of as all of God's commandments contained in the 66 books of the Bible in a nutshell. Each of the Ten Commandments has deep spiritual meaning in it. When we understand the true meaning of each and abide by it, God calls us righteous.

Jesus said there is the great and foremost commandment. It is to love God with all our heart, soul, and mind. The second is to love our neighbor as ourselves (Matthew 22:37-39).

Jesus kept and practiced all these commandments. He never quarreled or cried out. Jesus prayed all the time, whether early in the morning or all through the night. He kept all the statutes, too. 'Statutes' refer to the rules that God set forth for us, as in keeping the Passover or giving tithes. There is a record of Jesus going up to Jerusalem to observe the Passover, just like all the other Jews.

Christians, who are spiritual Jews, continue to preserve and observe the spiritual meanings of the Jewish rituals. Christians circumcise their hearts just as physical circumcision was done in the Old Testament times. They worship in spirit and truth in worship services, keeping the spiritual meaning of giving sacrifices to God in the Old Testament. When we keep God's laws and put them into practice, we come to receive true life and become righteous. The Lord overcame death and resurrected; therefore we can also enjoy eternal life by coming forth to the resurrection of righteousness.

The blessings for the righteous

Strife, enmities, and illnesses come because people are not righteous. Lawlessness comes from not being righteous, and then come pain and suffering. This is because people receive the work of the devil, the father of sins. If there was no lawlessness and no unrighteousness, there would be no catastrophes, suffering, or hardships, and this world would truly be a beautiful place. Furthermore, if you become a righteous person in God's eyes, you will receive great blessings from Him. You can become a truly outstanding and blessed person.

Deuteronomy 28:1-6 talks about it in detail: *"Now it shall be, if you diligently obey the LORD your God, being careful to do all His commandments which I command you today, the LORD your God will set you high above all the nations of the earth. All these blessings will come upon you and overtake you if you obey the LORD your God: Blessed shall you be in the city, and blessed shall you be in the country. Blessed shall be the offspring of your body and the produce of your ground and the offspring of your beasts, the increase of your herd and the young of your flock. Blessed shall be your basket and your kneading bowl. Blessed shall you be when you come in, and blessed shall you be when you go out."*

Also, in Exodus 15:26 God promised that if we do what is right in God's sight, He would put none of the diseases on us which He had put on the Egyptians. Therefore if we do what is righteous in God's eyes, then we will be healthy. We can prosper in all areas of our lives and experience eternal joy and blessings.

So far we looked at what righteousness in God's eyes is. Now, by acting in accordance with God's laws and statutes without blemish, and living righteously in God's sight, I hope you can experience God's love and blessings to the full measure!

Glossary

Faith and the righteous

There are two types of faith: 'spiritual faith' and 'fleshly faith'. Having **'fleshly faith'** is only being able to believe in the things that coincide with one's knowledge and thoughts. This type of faith is faith without action; therefore it is a dead faith which God does not acknowledge. Having **'spiritual faith'** is being able to believe in everything that comes from the Word of God, even though it may not coincide with one's knowledge or thoughts. With this type of faith, a person acts according to God's Word.

One can only have this kind of faith if God gives it to him, and each person has a different measure of faith (Romans 12:3). Largely, faith can be categorized from level one through five: at the first level of faith, one has the faith to receive salvation, at the second level, one tries to act according to God's Word, at the third level, one can fully act according to the Word, at the fourth level, one has become sanctified by casting away sins, and loves the Lord with his utmost, and at the fifth level, one has the faith to bring complete joy to God.

'The righteous' refers to persons who are righteous.

When we accept Jesus Christ and are forgiven of our sins through His precious blood, we are justified. This means we are justified by our faith. Now when we cast out the evil—or untruths—from our hearts and we strive to act in the truth, according to God's Word, we can transform into truly righteous people, who are acknowledged by God as righteous. God takes great joy in righteous people like these, and He answers their every prayer (James 5:16).

Chapter 7

The Righteous Shall Live By Faith

"For in it the righteousness of God is revealed from faith to faith; as it is written, 'But the righteous man shall live by faith.'"
(Romans 1:17)

When someone does a good deed for an orphan, a widow, or a neighbor in need, more often than not, people will call that person a righteous man or woman. When someone appears to be gentle and kind, abides by the law, does not get angry easily, and is quietly patient, people compliment the person saying, "That person doesn't even need rules." So does this really mean this person is righteous?

Hosea 14:9 says, *"Whoever is wise, let him understand these things; whoever is discerning, let him know them. For the ways of the LORD are right, and the righteous will walk in them, but transgressors will stumble in them."* It means a person who abides by the laws of God is a truly righteous person.

Also, Luke 1:5-6 says, *"In the days of Herod, king of*

Judea, there was a priest named Zacharias, of the division of Abijah; and he had a wife from the daughters of Aaron, and her name was Elizabeth. They were both righteous in the sight of God, walking blamelessly in all the commandments and requirements of the Lord."* This means that someone is righteous only when he practices the laws of God, namely all the commandments and statutes of the Lord.

To become a truly righteous person

No matter how hard one tries to be righteous, nobody is righteous because everyone has original sin, which is passed on from his ancestors, and self-committed sins, or otherwise known as actual sins. Romans 3:10 says, *"There is none righteous, not even one."* The one and only righteous man was, and is, Jesus Christ.

Jesus, who had neither original sin nor self-committed sins, shed His blood and died on the cross to pay for the penalty of our sins, and He rose again from the dead and became our Savior. The moment we believe in Jesus Christ, who is the way, the truth, and the life, that is when our sins are washed away, and we are justified. However, just because we are justified by faith, that does not mean we're done. Yes, when we believe in Jesus Christ, we are forgiven of our sins and are justified; however, we still have sinful natures inside of our hearts.

This is why in Romans 2:13 it is written, *"For it is not the hearers of the Law who are just before God, but the doers of the Law will be justified."* It means even though we are justified by faith, we can become a truly righteous person only when we change the heart of untruth into the heart of truth by acting according to the Word of God.

In the Old Testament times, before the Holy Spirit came, people could not completely cast off their sins on their own. So if they did not sin with their actions, they were not considered sinners. This was the time of the Law, where people were paid back 'an eye for an eye, and a tooth for a tooth'. However, what God wants is the circumcision of the heart—casting out the untruth, or sinful natures of the heart, and practicing love and mercy. So unlike the people of Old Testament times, people of the New Testament times who accept Jesus Christ receive the Holy Spirit as a gift, and with the help of the Holy Spirit, they are empowered to cast out the sinful natures from their hearts. Man cannot cast out sin and become righteous with his own power alone. This is why the Holy Spirit came.

Therefore, in order to become a truly righteous person, we need the help of the Holy Spirit. When we cry out to God in our prayers in order to become righteous, God gives us grace and strength, and the Holy Spirit helps us. So we can definitely overcome sin and pull out the sinful natures by its roots from within our hearts! As we increasingly cast out sin, become sanctified, and reach the full measure of faith with the help of the Holy Spirit, we receive more of God's love and become truly righteous people.

Why do we need to become righteous?

You may ask, "Do I really need to become righteous? Can't I just believe in Jesus to a certain point and live a normal life?" But God says in Revelations 3:15-16, *"I know your deeds, that you are neither cold nor hot; I wish that you were cold or hot. So because you are lukewarm, and neither hot nor cold, I will spit you out of My mouth."*

God does not like 'average faith'. Lukewarm faith is dangerous, because it is really hard to keep this kind of faith over a long period of time. Ultimately, this type of faith becomes cold. It's just like warm water. If you leave it out for a while, it eventually cools down and becomes cold. God says He will spit out people with this kind of faith. This means that people with this type of faith cannot be saved.

So then why do we need to be righteous? As it is written in Romans 6:23, *"For the wages of sin is death",* a sinner belongs to the enemy, the devil and walks to the way of death. Therefore the sinner has to turn away from sin and become righteous. Only then can a sinner become free from the trials, tribulations, and illnesses that the devil gives him. As man lives on in this world, he is very likely to experience all kinds of sad and difficult situations such as sicknesses, accidents and deaths. However, if one becomes righteous, he has nothing to do with these things.

Therefore, we need to take heed to God's words and keep all His commandments. If we live righteously, we can receive all the blessings described in Deuteronomy chapter 28. And as our soul prospers, we will prosper in all respects, and we will be healthy.

But until you become a righteous person who is able to receive all these blessings, hardships will follow. For example, in order to win a gold medal at the Olympics, athletes go through rigorous training. Like so, little by little, God will allow His loving children to undergo certain trials and tribulations within the scope of their ability according to their measure of faith, so their soul will increasingly prosper.

God told Abraham to leave his father's house and said, *"Walk before Me and be blameless"* (Genesis 17:1). He trained him and led him to become a truly righteous man. Ultimately, after Abraham passed the last test to sacrifice his only son, Isaac, as a burnt offering to God, the trials were over. After that, Abraham was blessed all the time, and everything always went well with him.

God trains us to increase our faith and make us righteous. When each person passes each trial, God blesses him, and then leads him to even greater faith. And through this process, we cultivate the heart of the Lord increasingly.

The glory that we receive in Heaven will vary, depending on how much of our sins we cast out, and how much our hearts resemble that of Christ. Just as it is written in 1 Corinthians 15: 41, *"There is one glory of the sun, and another glory of the moon, and another glory of the stars; for star differs from star in glory,"* the magnitude of glory we get in Heaven depends on how righteous we become in this world.

The kind of children God wants to have are those who have the true qualifications of His children—those that have the heart of the Lord. These people will enter into the New Jerusalem where God's throne is, and they will get to dwell in a place of glory that shines like the sun.

The righteous shall live by faith

So how should we live, in order to become a righteous person? We need to live by faith, as it is written in Romans 1:17, *"But the righteous man shall live by faith."* We can divide faith into two major categories: fleshly faith and spiritual faith. Fleshly faith is faith based on knowledge or faith based on reason.

When a man is born and raised, the things he sees, hears, and learns from his parents, teachers, neighbors and friends become stored as knowledge in a memory device in his brain. If a person believes only when something coincides with the knowledge that he already has, this is called fleshly faith. People who have this type of faith believe something can be created from something that already exists. But they cannot believe in or accept creation of something from nothing.

For example, they cannot believe that God created the heavens and the earth with Word. They cannot believe the incident where Jesus calmed the storm by rebuking the wind and commanding the sea, *"Be still"* (Mark 4:39). God opened the mouth of a donkey and made him speak. He had Moses part the Red Sea with his staff. He even made the massive wall of Jericho crumble down after the Israelites simply marched around it and shouted. These events do not make sense at all, according to the average person's knowledge and reasoning.

How can the sea be parted, just because someone lifts up a staff toward it? However, if God—for whom nothing is impossible—makes it happen, it happens! A person who confesses to believe in God and yet does not have spiritual faith will not believe these events really took place. So a person who has fleshly faith does not have the faith to believe, so naturally, they cannot obey God's Word. Therefore they cannot receive answers to their prayers, and they cannot receive salvation. This is why their faith is called 'dead faith'.

On the contrary, spiritual faith—the faith to believe in the creation of something from nothing—is called 'living faith'.

Those with this type of faith will break down their thoughts of the flesh, and they will not try to understand an incident or situation solely based on their own knowledge and thoughts. Those with spiritual faith have the faith to accept everything in the Bible simply the way it is. Spiritual faith is the faith that believes in the impossible. And because it leads man to salvation, it is called 'living faith'. If you want to become righteous, you must possess spiritual faith.

How to possess spiritual faith

In order to possess spiritual faith, we must first get rid of all the thoughts and theories in our mind that distract us from obtaining spiritual faith. As it is written in 2 Corinthians 10:5, we must destroy speculations and every lofty thing raised up against the knowledge of God, and we must make every thought captive to the obedience of Christ.

The knowledge, theories, intellection, and values that a person learns from birth are not always true. Only the Word of God is the absolute and everlasting truth. If we persist that our limited human knowledge and theories are true, then there is no way we can accept God's Word as truth. Thus, we won't be able to possess spiritual faith. That is why it is so important for us to break down this type of mindset, first and foremost.

Also, in order to possess spiritual faith, we must diligently listen to the Words of God. Romans 10:17 says that faith comes from *hearing*; therefore we must *hear* God's Word. If we don't hear the words of God, we won't know what truth is—so spiritual faith cannot take place in us. As we hear the words of

God or the testimonies of other people in worship services and various church meetings, sprout of faith grows inside of us, even though it might be faith as knowledge at first.

Then, in order to transform this knowledge-based faith into spiritual faith, we need to practice the words of God. As it is written in James 2:22, faith works with man's works, and as a result of the works, faith is perfected.

A person who loves baseball cannot become a great baseball player just because he reads many books about baseball. If he gathered the knowledge, he must now go through rigorous training according to the knowledge he acquired, in order to become a great baseball player. In the same way, no matter how much you read the Bible, if your actions do not follow what you read, your faith will only remain as knowledge-based faith, and you will not be able to possess spiritual faith. When you put what you heard into action, this is when God gives you spiritual faith—the faith to truly believe from the center of your heart.

So then, if someone truly believes from his heart the word of God that says, *"Rejoice always; pray without ceasing; in everything give thanks"*, what kind of actions would he take? Of course, he will rejoice in joyful circumstances. But he will also rejoice when tough situations arise. With joy, he will commit everything into God's hands. No matter how busy he might be, he will take time to pray. And no matter what the circumstances may be, he will always give thanks, believing his prayers will be answered, because he believes in the Almighty God.

In this way, when we obey God's words, God is pleased with our faith, and He takes away the trials and tribulations and answers our prayers so that, indeed, we do have reasons to be joyful and give thanks. When we pray diligently, cast out the untruths from our heart with the help of the Holy Spirit, and we act according to God's Word, then our knowledge-based faith becomes like a pedestal upon which God gives us spiritual faith.

If we have spiritual faith, we will obey the Word of God. When we try, with faith, to put into action something we cannot do, then God helps us to do it. This is why receiving financial blessings should be very easy. As it is recorded in Malachi 3:10, when we give whole tithes, God pours so much blessing upon us that our storehouse will overflow! Because we believe that when we sow, we will reap 30, 60, 100 times, we can sow with joy. This is how, with faith, the righteous receive God's love and blessings.

Ways to live by faith

In our daily lives, we come across the 'Red Sea' that stands before us, 'The City of Jericho' that we must tear down, and 'Jordan River' that floods. When these problems come before us, walking in the truth is living by faith. For example, with fleshly faith, if someone strikes us we would want to strike back and hate the other person. But if we have spiritual faith, we would not hate the other person, but rather love him. When we have this kind of living faith—the faith to put God's Word into action—the enemy devil flees from us, and our problems are resolved.

The righteous who live by faith will love God, obey and keep His commandments, and act according to the truth. Once in a while people ask, "How can we keep all the commandments?" As it is only proper for a child to honor his parents, and for a husband and wife to love one another, if we call ourselves children of God, it is only proper for us to keep His commands.

For new believers who just began attending church, it might be hard at first to close their shop on Sundays. They hear that God will bless them if they keep the whole Sabbath by closing their shop on Sundays, but it may be hard to believe at first. So in some cases, they may just attend the Sunday morning service and then open their shop in the afternoon.

On the other hand, for more mature believers, profit is not a problem for them. Their first priority is to obey God's Word, so they obey by closing their shop on Sunday. Then God sees their faith and makes sure they make much more profit than the profit they make when they open their shop on Sundays. As God promised, He will protect them from loss, and He will bless them pressed down, shaken together, and running over.

This also applies to casting out sins. Sins like hate, jealousy, and lust are hard to cast out, but they can be cast out when we pray fervently. From my personal experience, with sins that could not be cast out simply with prayer, I cast them out with fasting. If fasting for three days didn't work, I fasted five days. If that still didn't work, I tried seven days, and then ten days. I fasted until the sin was cast out. Then, I found myself casting out sin to avoid fasting!

If we can cast away those couple of sins that are the most difficult to cast away, then the other sins are easy to cast away. It's like pulling out a tree by its roots. If we pull out the main root, all the other little roots come out with it.

If we love God, keeping His commandments is not difficult. How can someone who loves God not obey His words? Loving God is obeying His words. So if you have love for Him, you can keep all of His commandments. Are the problems piled up before you as big as the Red Sea or as formidable as the city of Jericho?

If we possess spiritual faith, put our faith into action, and walk in the way of righteousness, then God will solve all of our difficult problems and take our suffering away. The more righteous we become, the faster our problems become resolved, and the speedier our prayers are answered! So finally, I hope that you will enjoy a flourishing life not only in this world, but also eternal blessings in Heaven as well by marching on with faith as a righteous person of God!

Glossary

Thoughts, Theories, and Frameworks of the Mind

'Thought' is, through the operation of soul, to bring out the knowledge stored in the memory device of the brain. These thoughts can be categorized into two parts: fleshly thoughts that are against God, and spiritual thoughts which please God. Among the knowledge that is stored in our memory, if we choose that which is truth, we will have spiritual thoughts. On the contrary, if we choose that which is untruth, we will have fleshly thoughts.

'Theory' is logic that one establishes based on the knowledge that is acquired through his experience, intellection, or education. Theory varies depending on each person's experience, thoughts, or era. It creates disputes, and many times goes against the Word of God.

'Framework' is the mental frameworks with which one believes he is right. These frameworks are made as a person's self-righteousness is hardened. For this reason, for some people their personality itself becomes frameworks, and for some others, their knowledge and theories can become frameworks. We must hear the Word of God and understand the truth in order to discover these frameworks in our minds and tear them down.

Chapter 8

To the Obedience of Christ

"For though we walk in the flesh, we do not war according to the flesh, for the weapons of our warfare are not of the flesh, but divinely powerful for the destruction of fortresses. We are destroying speculations and every lofty thing raised up against the knowledge of God, and we are taking every thought captive to the obedience of Christ, and we are ready to punish all disobedience, whenever your obedience is complete."
(2 Corinthians 10:3-6)

If we accept Jesus Christ, and become a righteous man who possesses spiritual faith, we can receive unbelievable blessings from God. Not only can we give glory to God by doing the work of God in a mighty way, but whatever we ask for in prayer, He will answer us and we can lead lives that are prosperous in all ways.

However, there are some people who confess to believe in God, and yet do not obey God's Word, and therefore cannot achieve the righteousness of God. They profess to pray and work hard for the Lord, and yet they do not receive blessings, and they are constantly in the midst of trials, tribulations, and illnesses. If one has faith, one should live according to God's Word and receive His abundant blessings. But why are believers not able to do this? It is because they continue to hold on to the fleshly thoughts.

Fleshly thoughts which are hostile toward God

The term "flesh" refers to one's body combined with sinful natures. These sinful natures are the untruths that are in one's heart, which have not been outwardly revealed as action. When these untruths come out in the form of thoughts, these thoughts are called "fleshly thoughts". When we have fleshly thoughts, we cannot obey the truth completely. Romans 8:7 says, *"...because the mind set on the flesh is hostile toward God; for it does not subject itself to the law of God, for it is not even able to do so."*

Then, more specifically, what are these fleshly thoughts? There are two types of thoughts. The first are spiritual thoughts which help us act according to the truth, or God's laws, and the other are fleshly thoughts which keep us from acting according to God's laws (Romans 8:6). By choosing between truth and untruth, we can either have spiritual thoughts or fleshly thoughts.

Sometimes when we see someone we do not like, on the one hand, we may have thoughts of disliking that person according to our ill-feelings toward him. On the other hand, we might have thoughts of trying to love that person. If we see our neighbor who has something really nice, we could have the thought of stealing it from him or the thought that we must not covet our neighbor's possessions. Thoughts that are in accordance with the law of God that says "Love your neighbor", and "Do not covet", these are spiritual thoughts. But thoughts that provoke you to hate and steal are contrary to God's laws; and are thus fleshly thoughts.

Fleshly thoughts are hostile toward God; therefore they stunt our spiritual growth and go against God. If we follow fleshly thoughts, we grow distant from God, succumb to the secular world, and ultimately come to face trials and tribulations. There are many things that we see, hear, and learn from this world. Many of them are against God's will and are a distraction to our walk in faith. We have to realize that these things are all fleshly thoughts that are hostile toward God. And once we discover those thoughts, we need to cast them out thoroughly. No matter how right it seems to you , if it is not in line with God's will, it is a fleshly thought, and therefore hostile toward God.

Let's consider the case of Peter. When Jesus told the disciples about how He will have to go up to Jerusalem to be crucified and then resurrect on the third day, Peter said, *"God forbid it, Lord! This shall never happen to You"* (Matthew 16:22). But then Jesus said, *"Get behind Me, Satan! You are a stumbling block to Me; for you are not setting your mind on God's interests, but man's"* (Matthew 16:23).

As Jesus' right-hand disciple, Peter said this out of love for his teacher. But no matter how good his intention was, his words went against God's will. Because it was God's will for Him to take up the cross and open the door to salvation, Jesus cast away Satan, who was trying to distract Peter through his thoughts.

Ultimately, as he experienced Jesus' death and resurrection, Peter came to realize how worthless and hostile fleshly thoughts are toward God, and he completely destroyed those thoughts. As a result, Peter became the key player in spreading the gospel of Christ and building up the first church to be firm.

"Self-Righteousness" – one of the prime fleshly thoughts

Among all the different types of fleshly thoughts, "self-righteousness" is a prime example. Simply put, "self-righteousness" is arguing that you are right. After a person is born, he learns many things from his parents and teachers. He also learns things through friends and the various environments one is exposed to.

But no matter how great a person's parents and teachers may be, it is not easy for one to learn solely the truth. It is more likely that he learns many things that go against the will of God. Of course everyone tries to teach what he or she thinks is correct; however, when reflected upon God's standard of righteousness, almost all things are untruth. Very little is of the truth. This is because no one is good except for God alone (Mark 10:18; Luke 18:19).

For example, God tells us to repay evil with good. He tells us if someone forces you to go one mile with him, go with him two miles. If they take away your coat, give them your shirt as well. He teaches us that the one who serves is greater; and that the one who gives and sacrifices is the true victor in the end. But what people think of as 'righteousness' is different from person to person. They teach we must pay back evil with evil, and we have to stand up against evil to the bitter end until we defeat it.

Here's a simple illustration. Your child goes over to his friend's house and comes back home crying. His face looks like it's been scratched by someone's finger nails. At this point, most parents become very upset and begin chastising their child. In some serious cases, the parent may say, "Next time, don't just sit there and take it. Fight back!" They are teaching their child that getting beat up is a sign of weakness, or losing.

Also, there are those people who may be suffering from an illness. Regardless of how their caretaker may feel, they demand this and demand that, trying to make themselves more comfortable. From the sick person's standpoint, because their pain is great they think their actions are justified. However, God teaches us not to seek the benefit of ourselves, but to seek the benefit of others. This is how man's thoughts and God's thoughts are different. Man's standard of righteousness and God's standard of righteousness are very different.

In Genesis 37:2, we see Joseph, who, out of his own righteousness was pointing out wrongdoings of his brothers to his father from time to time. From his standpoint, he didn't like the lawlessness of his brothers' actions. If Joseph had had a little bit more goodness in his heart, he would have sought for God's wisdom and found a better and more peaceful solution to the problem without discomforting his brothers. However, because of his self-righteousness, he was hated by his brothers, and by their hands he was sold into slavery to Egypt. So in this way, if you offend another person because of what you think is 'righteous', then you may experience this type of tribulation.

However, what happened to Joseph, after he realized the righteousness of God through the trials and tribulations he faced? He cast out his self-righteousness and rose to the position of Prime Minister of Egypt and earned the authority to rule over many people. He even saved his family from a great famine including even his brothers, the ones who had sold him into slavery. He also was used to provide the foundation for the formation of the nation of Israel.

Apostle Paul broke down his fleshly thoughts

In Philippians 3:7-9, Paul said, *"But whatever things were gain to me, those things I have counted as loss for the sake of Christ. More than that, I count all things to be loss in view of the surpassing value of knowing Christ Jesus my Lord, for whom I have suffered the loss of all things, and count them but rubbish so that I may gain Christ, and may be found in Him..."*

Born in Tarsus, the capital of Cilicia, Paul was a Roman citizen by birth. Having the citizenship of Rome that ruled the world at that time means that he had considerable social power. In addition to this, Paul was an orthodox Pharisee from the tribe of Benjamin (Acts 22:3), and he studied under Gamaliel, the best scholar of that time.

As the most zealous of Jews, Paul was at the forefront of persecuting the Christians. In fact, he was actually on his way to Damascus to arrest the Christians that were there, when he met Jesus Christ. Through this encounter with the Lord, Paul realized his wrongdoing and came to know for sure that Jesus Christ is indeed the true Savior. From that moment forth, he denied his education, values, and social status and followed the Lord.

After meeting Jesus Christ, what is the reason that Paul counted as loss all those things that were gain to him? He realized that all his knowledge came from man, a mere creature, and therefore was very limited. He also came to know that man can gain life and enjoy eternal happiness in Heaven by believing in God and accepting Jesus Christ, and that the beginning of knowledge and all understanding is, in fact, God.

Paul realized that the scholarly knowledge of this world is merely necessary for living in this world, but the knowledge of Jesus Christ is the noblest form of knowledge which can solve man's fundamental problem. He discovered that within the knowledge of knowing Jesus Christ, there is limitless power and authority, treasures, honor, and riches. Because he had such firm belief in this fact, he counted as loss and rubbish all his scholarly knowledge and understanding from this world. This was in order to gain Christ and be found in Him.

If someone is headstrong and thinks, "I know", and he is full of himself, thinking, "I am always right", then he would never be able to discover his true self, and will always think he is the best. This type of person will not listen to others with a humble heart; therefore he cannot learn anything, and he cannot understand anything. However, Paul met Jesus Christ, the greatest teacher of all time. And in order to make His teachings his own, he cast off all of his fleshly thoughts which he once considered as absolutely right. This was because Paul had to get rid of his fleshly thoughts in order to gain the noble knowledge of Christ.

Therefore, the apostle Paul was able to achieve the

righteousness that pleased God, as he confessed, *"...not having a righteousness of my own derived from the Law, but that which is through faith in Christ, the righteousness which comes from God on the basis of faith"* (Philippians 3:9).

The righteousness which comes from God

Before meeting the Lord, the apostle Paul kept the Law strictly and he considered himself to be righteous. But after meeting the Lord and receiving the Holy Spirit, he discovered his true self and confessed, *"Christ Jesus came into the world to save sinners, among whom I am foremost of all"* (1 Timothy 1:15). He had realized that he had both original sin and self-committed sins/actual sins, and that he was yet to fulfill true, spiritual love. If, from the beginning he had been righteous and had he walked in the faith that pleased God, he would have recognized who Jesus was and served Him from the start. However, he did not recognize the Savior, and instead he took part in persecuting those that believed in Jesus. So in all reality, he was no different from the Pharisees that nailed Jesus to the cross.

In the Old Testament times, they had to pay back an eye for an eye and a tooth for a tooth. According to the Law, if someone committed murder or adultery, he was stoned to death. But the Pharisees did not understand the true heart of God contained in the Law. Why would a God of love create rules like that?

In the Old Testament times, the Holy Spirit did not come in the hearts of the people. It was harder for them to control their actions than those who have received the Holy Spirit, the Helper, in the New Testament times. Thus, sin could spread very quickly if there was no retribution but only forgiveness. For this reason, in order to prevent people from committing sins and to prevent sins from spreading, they had to pay life for life, an eye for an eye, a tooth for a tooth, and a foot for a foot. Also, murder and adultery are seriously evil sins, merely by the secular standard, too. A person who commits these types of sins has a heart that is very hardened. It would be very difficult for a person like this to turn from his ways. So, since he can't receive salvation, and he is going to Hell anyway, it would be better for him to be stoned and let that punishment serve as a warning and lesson for other people.

This is God's love, too, but God never intended or desired for man to have a legalistic form of faith where one had to pay eye for an eye, and a tooth for a tooth. In Deuteronomy 10:16, God said, *"So circumcise your heart, and stiffen your neck no longer."* And Jeremiah 4:4 says, *"Circumcise yourselves to the LORD and remove the foreskins of your heart, men of Judah and inhabitants of Jerusalem, or else My wrath will go forth like fire and burn with none to quench it, because of the evil of your deeds."*

You can see that even in the Old Testament times, those prophets that God acknowledged did not have legalistic faith. This is because what God truly wants is spiritual love and compassion. Just as Jesus Christ fulfilled the Law with love, those prophets and patriarchs that received God's love and blessings sought after love and peace.

In Moses' case, when the sons of Israel stood at the brink of death by committing an unforgivable sin, He interceded on their behalf asking God to exchange his salvation for theirs. Paul, however, was not like this before he met Jesus Christ. He was not righteous in God's eyes. He was righteous in his own eyes.

Only after meeting Christ did he consider as loss everything he knew before, and he began to spread the noble knowledge of Christ. Out of his love for souls, Paul planted churches wherever he stepped, and he sacrificed his life for the gospel. He lived a most valuable and worthy kind of life.

Saul disobeyed God with fleshly thoughts

Saul is the prime example of a man who set himself up against God because of his fleshly thoughts. Anointed by the Prophet Samuel, Saul was the first king of Israel who ruled the nation for 40 years. Before he became the king, he was a humble man. But after becoming the king, he slowly became more and more proud. For example, when Israel was getting ready to go to war with the Philistines and Prophet Samuel did not come at the appointed time, and the people began to scatter, even though only the priest was supposed to make the sacrifice at the altar, Saul made the sacrifice himself, on his own accord, acting against the will of God. And when Samuel chastised him for having no regard for the sacred boundaries of the priest, instead of repenting, Saul was quick to make excuses.

And when God told him to 'completely destroy the Amalekites', he did not obey. He captured the king instead. He even spared the choice livestock and brought them back home. Because he allowed his fleshly thoughts to creep in, he put his own thoughts before God's words. And yet he asked his people to raise him up. Finally, God turned His face away from him, and he was tormented by evil spirits. But even under these circumstances, he refused to turn away from evil, and he attempted to kill David, the one God had anointed. God gave Saul many chances to make a turnabout, but he could not cast off his fleshly thoughts, and once again, he disobeyed God. Ultimately, he went to the way of death.

The way to fulfill God's righteousness through faith

Then how can we cast out fleshly thoughts which are hostile toward God and become righteous in the sight of God? We must destroy all speculations and every lofty thing raised up against the knowledge of God, and take every thought captive to the obedience of Christ (2 Corinthians 10:5).

Obeying Christ does not mean being shackled or being afflicted. It is the way to blessings and eternal life. This is why those who have accepted Jesus Christ as their Savior and experienced the amazing love of God obey His Word and strive to emulate His heart.

So, in order to achieve the righteousness of God through faith in Jesus Christ, we need to cast away every form of evil (1 Thessalonians 5:22) and seek to accomplish goodness. You will not have fleshly thoughts if you do not have untruths in your heart. You receive the work of Satan and go the evil way as much as you have untruth in you. Therefore, obeying Christ means casting out untruths from within us and knowing and acting in accordance to God's Word.

If God tells us to "devote ourselves to meeting together", then without involving our own thoughts, we should devote ourselves to meeting together. As we attend worship services, we should understand God's ways and obey accordingly. However, just because we know the Word of God does not mean we can put it all into practice right away. We must pray in order to receive the strength to put the Word into action. When we pray, we become full of the Holy Spirit, and can cut off fleshly thoughts. But if we do not pray, our fleshly thoughts will take hold of us and lead us astray.

Therefore, we should pray while diligently striving to live according to God's Word. Before we met Jesus Christ, we might have followed the desires of the flesh saying, 'let's rest, enjoy, let's drink and eat and be merry'. But after meeting Jesus Christ, we should meditate on how we can fulfill His kingdom and His righteousness, and we should work hard to put our faith into action. We should discover and cast out evils such as hate and jealousy which are contrary to God's Word. We should do as Jesus did—loving our enemies and lowering ourselves while serving others. Then, this means we are achieving the righteousness of God.

I hope that you will be able to destroy speculations and every lofty thing raised up against the knowledge of God, and take every thought captive to the obedience of Christ just as the apostle Paul did, so that you will receive wisdom and understanding from God and become a righteous person who is prosperous in all things.

Glossary

The Righteousness of Faith, Obedience, and Deeds

Righteousness of faith is seeing the positive outcome with eyes of faith instead of simply seeing the reality as it is by trusting in God's Word. It is relying not on one's own thoughts and abilities, but on God's Word alone.

Righteousness of obedience is not just obeying a command that one can carry out with his or her own strength. It is, within the boundary of truth, obeying even a command that one thinks is impossible to carry out. If a person has righteousness of faith he can also fulfill the righteousness of obedience. A person who has fulfilled the righteousness of obedience based on his righteousness of faith can obey with faith, even in circumstances that are realistically impossible.

Righteousness of deeds is the ability to act according to God's will without making any excuses, as long as it is something God wants. The capacity to carry out righteousness of deeds varies with each person depending on each one's character of vessel and character of heart. The more a person disregards their own benefit and seeks for the benefit of others, the more one can fulfill this type of righteousness.

Chapter 9

He Whom the Lord Commends

"For it is not he who commends himself that is approved, but he whom the Lord commends."
(2 Corinthians 10:18)

No matter what field we are in, if we excel at what we do, we can be commended. However, there is a difference between being commended by some random person, and being commended by an expert in the field you are in. So if our Lord, the King of kings, the Lord of lords acknowledges us, then that joy would not be incomparable to anything in this world!

He whom the Lord commends

God commends those people whose hearts are righteous, and who bear the aroma of Christ. In the Bible, there aren't too many cases where Jesus extends commendation. But when He did, it was not forthright but He did it indirectly in wording such as, "You have done the right thing." "Remember this." "Spread this."

In Luke chapter 21, we see a poor widow making an offering of two small copper coins. Jesus commended this widow for making an offering with everything she had, saying, *"Truly I say to you, this poor widow put in more than all of them; for they all out of their surplus put into the offering; but she out of her poverty put in all that she had to live on"* (vv. 3-4).

In Mark chapter 14, we encounter the scene where a woman pours expensive perfume on Jesus' head. Some people that were there scolded her for this, saying, *"This perfume might have been sold for over three hundred denarii, and the money given to the poor"* (v. 5).

At this, Jesus said, *"You always have the poor with you, and whenever you wish you can do good to them; but you do not always have Me. She has done what she could; she has anointed My body beforehand for the burial. Truly I say to you, wherever the gospel is preached in the whole world, what this woman has done will also be spoken of in memory of her"* (vv. 6-9).

If you wish to be commended by the Lord like this, then you must first do what you ought to do. So then, let's study more specifically about those things that we ought to do as people of God.

To be approved by God

1) Diligently build an altar before God

Genesis 12:7-8 says, *"The LORD appeared to Abram and said, 'To your descendants I will give this land.' So he built an altar there to the LORD who had appeared to him. Then he proceeded from there to the mountain on the east of Bethel, and pitched his tent, with Bethel on the west and Ai on the east; and there he built an altar to the LORD and called upon the name of the LORD."* Furthermore, in Genesis 13:4 and 13:18, it is also recorded that Abraham built an altar before God.

In Genesis chapter 28 we see the record of how Jacob built an altar before God. While fleeing from his brother who was trying to kill him, Jacob came upon a place where he fell asleep with a rock under his head. In his dream, he saw a ladder reaching to heaven, and he saw the angels of God going up and down the ladder, and he heard the voice of God. When he woke up the next morning, Jacob took the rock he was using as a pillow, raised it up like a pillar, poured oil over it, and praised God there.

In today's terms, building an altar before God is equivalent to going to church and attending worship services. It is making a genuine offering with all our heart while giving thanks; it is listening to God's Word and taking it in as nourishment for our heart. It is taking the word that we heard and putting it into action. In this way, as we worship in spirit and in truth, and as we practice the Word, God is pleased with us and leads us to a life of blessings.

2) Lift up prayers that God wants to hear

Prayer is spiritual breathing. It is communicating with God. The importance of prayer is emphasized in many different places throughout the Bible. Of course even if we don't tell Him every minute detail, He knows everything already. However, because He wants to communicate with us and share love with us, God made this promise in Matthew 7:7, *"Ask, and it will be given to you."*

In order for our soul to prosper and go to Heaven, we need to pray. Only when we are filled with the grace and power of God and the fullness of the Holy Spirit, can we cast out fleshly thoughts that are contrary to the truth and can we become filled with God's Word, the truth. Also, we need to pray in order to become a man of truth, a man of spirit. By praying, all things will prosper with us and we will be in good health as our soul also prospers.

All the people that were loved and acknowledged by God were people who prayed. 1 Samuel 12:23 says, *"Far be it from me that I should sin against the LORD by ceasing to pray."* In order to receive something from God that is not possible with man's power, we need to communicate with God. Daniel, Peter, and the apostle Paul were all people who prayed. Jesus prayed early in the morning and sometimes all through the night. The story of how He prayed until His sweat became like drops of blood at Gethsemane is very famous.

3) Have the faith to receive answers

In Matthew chapter 8, a centurion comes to see Jesus. At the time Israel was occupied by Rome. A centurion of the Roman army would be equivalent to a higher ranking military officer today. The centurion asked Jesus to heal his servant who was suffering from paralysis. Jesus saw the love and faith of the centurion, so He decided to go heal the servant.

But the centurion made this confession of faith, *"Lord, I am not worthy for You to come under my roof, but just say the word, and my servant will be healed. For I also am a man under authority, with soldiers under me; and I say to this one, 'Go!' and he goes, and to another, 'Come!' and he comes, and to my slave, 'Do this!' and he does it"* (Matthew 9:8-9).

Seeing the centurion's faith and humbleness as very precious, Jesus said, *"Truly I say to you, I have not found such great faith with anyone in Israel."* (v. 10). Many people desire to have this kind of faith, but we cannot just have this kind of faith at our will. The more goodness we have in our heart and the more we put God's Word into action, that's how much of this kind of faith God gives us. Because the centurion had a good heart, what he saw and heard about Jesus, he just believed. In this way, God commends anyone who believes and puts his faith into action, and God works according to their faith.

4) Have a humble heart before God

In Mark chapter 7, a Syrophoenician woman came before Jesus with a humble heart, wishing for Him to heal her demon-possessed daughter. When the woman asked Him to heal her daughter, Jesus replied, *"Let the children be satisfied first, for it is not good to take the children's bread and throw it to the dogs"* (v. 27). The woman did not get angry or feel offended, even though she was being compared to a dog.

Because she was filled with a great desire to receive an answer no matter what, and because she believed in Jesus, who was the Truth itself, she lowered herself in a humble manner and she continued to cry out, *"Yes, Lord, but even the dogs under the table feed on the children's crumbs"* (v. 28). Jesus was moved by her faith and humility that He answered her request saying, *"Go; the demon has gone out of your daughter"* (v. 29). We need to have this kind of humility before God as we seek and pray.

5) Sow with faith

Sowing with faith is also a part of righteousness, which God commends. If you want to become wealthy, sow according to the law of sowing and reaping. This is most applicable when it comes to giving tithes and offerings of thanksgiving. Even when we look at the laws of nature, we can see that you reap what you sow. If you sow wheat, you will reap wheat, and if you sow beans, you will reap beans. If you sow a little, you will reap a little, and if you sow a lot, you will reap a lot. If you sow in fertile soil, you will reap good fruits; and the harder you prune and maintain, the choicer the crop you will reap.

The offering we make before God is used for saving lost souls, building churches, and supporting missions and helping the needy. This is why we can express our love of God through offerings. Offerings are used to fulfill God's kingdom and His righteousness, so God receives these offerings with joy and blesses us giving back 30, 60, or 100 fold. What would the Creator God lack that He would tell us to make offerings to Him? He is giving us the opportunity to reap what we sow and receive His blessings!

As it is written in 2 Corinthians 9:6-7, *"Now this I say, he who sows sparingly will also reap sparingly, and he who sows bountifully will also reap bountifully. Each one must do just as he has purposed in his heart, not grudgingly or under compulsion, for God loves a cheerful giver."*

6) Trust and rely on God at all times

David always inquired of God, so God led him on his path and helped him avoid various hardships. David asked God, "Shall I do this, or shall I do that?" specifically about almost everything, and he acted according to His direction (Ref: 1 Samuel chapter 23). That is why he was able to win so many battles. This is why God loves those of His children more who always trust and ask for His direction. However, if we call God 'Father', and yet trust the world or our own knowledge more than God, then God cannot help us.

The more we are in the truth, the more we can inquire of God and the more the Lord can commend us. In whatever we do, we should hone the wisdom of seeking God first and foremost, and then wait to receive His answer and guidance.

7) Obey God's Word

Because God commanded us, "Keep the Sabbath Day holy," we should go to church, worship, have fellowship with fellow believers, and spend the day in a holy way. And because He commanded us, "Rejoice always, and give thanks in everything," we should rejoice and be thankful no matter what circumstances come our way. People who keep His commands like these in their hearts and obey, receive the blessing of always being in God's presence.

Through obedience, Peter, Jesus' disciple, encountered an extraordinary event. In order to pay the temple taxes, Jesus told

Peter to *"go to the sea and throw in a hook, and take the first fish that comes up; and when you open its mouth, you will find a shekel. Take that and give it to them for you and Me"* (Matthew 17:27). If Peter refused to believe Jesus' words and did not go to the sea to catch the fish, then he wouldn't have experienced this wondrous event. But Peter obeyed and threw in the hook, and he was able to experience the awesome power of God.

All the works of faith recorded in the Bible are much in the same way. When God works He works according to each person's measure of faith. He will not push someone with a small measure of faith to submit beyond their ability. He first gives him the opportunity to experience His power by obeying something little, and then He gives him a little more spiritual faith through it. So the next time, he will be able to obey Him with something a little bigger.

Nail your passions and desires on the cross

So far we have studied about the things we must do in order to be acknowledged, commended, and be announced righteous before God. Furthermore, when we nail our fleshly passions and desires on the cross, God considers that as righteousness, and commends us. But why would passions and desires be considered sins? Galatians 5:24 writes, *"Now those who belong to Christ Jesus have crucified the flesh with its passions and desires."* It tells us that we should boldly cut off these things.

'Passion' is the giving and receiving one's heart. It is the closeness that you feel for someone as you get to know and build a relationship with him. This is not just true of two people courting one another, but also with family, friends, and neighbors. But because of these 'passions', we could easily become biased and narrow-minded. For example, most people are not as forgiving when a neighbor makes a small mistake, yet when their children make the same mistake, they are much more forgiving and understanding. But these kinds of fleshly passions do not help a nation, a family, or an individual to stand firm in righteousness.

'Desires' are the same way. Even David, who was so loved by God, ended up committing the grave sin of killing the innocent husband of Bathsheba, in order to hide the fact that he committed adultery with her. It is in these ways that fleshly passions and desires give birth to sin, and sin leads to the way of death. When sin is committed, the sinner will surely receive the retribution.

In Joshua chapter 7, we encounter the tragic event that occurred as a result of one man's fleshly desire. After the Exodus out of Egypt, during the process of conquering the land of Canaan, the Israelites crossed the Jordan River and gained a great triumph against the city of Jericho. After that, however, they were defeated in a battle against the city of Ai. When the Israelites looked into the cause of this defeat, they discovered that a man named Achan coveted and hid a mantle and some gold and silver from among the things seized from the city of Jericho. God had commanded the Israelites not to take anything they seized from Jericho for their personal gain, but Achan had disobeyed.

Because of Achan's sin, many Israelites had to suffer; and ultimately, Achan and his children were all stoned to death. Just as a small amount of leaven leavens the whole loaf, one man, Achan, could have caused the whole congregation of Israel to fail. That is why God dealt with him so severely. Our first thoughts might be, "How could God have someone put to death for stealing just one mantle and some pieces of gold and silver?" However, there is a rightful reason for what happened.

If a farmer, after he was done sowing, saw some weeds in the ground and thought, "Oh, it's just one or two..." and then left them alone, in no time, the weeds would grow and spread and choke out the crops. Then the farmer would not be able to reap good crops. Passions and desires are like weeds, so they become obstacles on the way to Heaven and the way to receiving answers from God. They are painful and futile distractions that serve no good purpose. This is why God tells us to 'nail these things to the cross'.

On the other hand, Asa, the third king of the southern kingdom of Judah, strictly cut off his passions and desires, thereby pleasing God (1 Kings chapter 15). Like his ancestor, David, Asa did what was right in the eyes of God, and rid his kingdom of all idols. When his mother, Maacah, created an image of Asherah, he went so far as to remove her from the position of queen mother. He then cut down the image and burned it at the Kidron brook.

You may think Asa was acting too extremely in removing his mother from being the queen mother just because she worshipped an idol, and you may even think Asa wasn't being a good son. However, Asa reacted this way because he asked his mother many times to stop worshipping idols. However, she did not listen to him. If we look at the situation through spiritual eyes, considering Maacah's position, her idol worship was like the whole nation worshipping the idol. This could ultimately bring God's wrath upon the entire nation. That is why God commended Asa's actions of cutting off his fleshly passion for his mother. He acknowledged it as righteous, to prevent many people from sinning against God.

Now this does not mean Asa disowned his mother. He simply removed her from the queen mother position. As her son, he continued to love, honor, and serve her. In the same way, if someone happens to have parents that worship false gods or idols, he should do all he can to touch their hearts by doing all that a son can do. From time to time, asking God for wisdom, he should share the gospel with them and encourage them to get rid of their idols. Then God will be pleased.

The patriarchs who were righteous before God

God commends complete obedience. He also shows His power to those that act in complete obedience. The kind of obedience that God acknowledges is obeying even when it seems impossible. In 2 Kings chapter 5, we see the record of the commander of the army of the king of Aram, Naaman.

General Naaman went into his neighboring country to visit the Prophet Elisha in hopes of being healed of leprosy. He took many gifts, even a letter from the king! However, when he got there, Elisha didn't even greet him. Instead, Elisha sent out a messenger to tell him to go wash in the Jordan River seven times.

Feeling quite offended, Naaman was ready to turn around and go back home. But at the persuasion of his servants, Naaman lowered his pride and obeyed. He washed his body in the Jordan River seven times. It must have been extremely difficult for the man second only to the king of Aram to let down his pride and obey like this, after being treated the way Elisha treated him.

Now Elisha did what he did because he knew that God would cure him after Naaman first showed his faith through obedience. God, who is pleased with our obedience as opposed to sacrifices, took joy in Naaman's act of faith and completely cured him of his leprosy. God considers obedience to be great in value, and He takes great joy in people who act in righteousness.

God also takes great joy in the faith of those people who do not seek their own benefit, and who do not compromise with the world. In Genesis chapter 23, when Abraham wanted to bury Sarah in the cave of Machpelah, the owner tried to give the land to Abraham for free. However, Abraham did not accept it. Abraham did not have the kind of heart that sought his own benefit. That is why he wanted to pay the exact price for the land before taking possession of it.

And when Sodom was defeated in war and his nephew Lot was captured, Abraham not only saved his nephew, but he also saved others that were from Sodom, and he brought back their possessions as well. When the king of Sodom tried to pay him back as a token of appreciation for what he did, Abraham refused. He did not accept anything. Because his heart was righteous, he did not have any greed, or the desire to take anything that didn't belong to him.

In Daniel chapter 6, we see Daniel knew full well that by

praying to God he would be killed because of those who had conspired against him. But nonetheless, he kept his righteousness before God by not ceasing to pray. He did not compromise even for a moment in order to save his own life. Because of his act, he was thrown into the lion's den. But he was unharmed, completely protected. He testified to the living God and glorified Him.

Even though he was wrongfully accused and put in jail for no reason, Joseph did not complain or hold resentment against anyone (Genesis chapter 39). He kept himself pure, did not compromise with untruth, and only followed the way of righteousness. So in God's time and way, he was freed from jail and rose to the honorary position of Prime Minister of Egypt.

So, we have to serve God, and we have to become righteous before God by doing what is required of us. We also have to please God by doing the things that the Lord will commend us for. When we do this, God will raise us up, answer the desires of our hearts and lead us in a prosperous life.

Glossary

The difference between 'Abram' and 'Abraham'

'Abram' is the original name of Abraham, the father of faith (Genesis 11:26).

'Abraham', meaning 'father of many nations', is the name God gave to Abram, in order to make a covenant of blessing with him (Genesis 17:5). Upon this covenant he became the source of blessing as the father of faith. And he was called a 'friend of God'.

Blessings that are pressed down, shaken together, and running over, and blessings of 30, 60, and 100 fold

We receive blessings from God according to the measure of how much we trust Him and put His Words into action in our lives. Even though we may not have cast out all the sinful natures from our hearts yet, when we sow and seek with faith, we receive blessings that are pressed down, shaken together, and running over, which is more than twice that we had sown (Luke 6:38). But if we become sanctified and go into spirit by struggling against sins to the point of shedding blood to cast them away completely, then we can reap blessings that are more than 30 fold. And if we go further into whole spirit, we can reap blessings that are 60, or even 100 fold.

Chapter 10

Blessing

> *"Now the LORD said to Abram, 'Go forth from your country, and from your relatives and from your father's house, to the land which I will show you; and I will make you a great nation, and I will bless you, and make your name great; and so you shall be a blessing; and I will bless those who bless you, and the one who curses you I will curse. and in you all the families of the earth will be blessed.' So Abram went forth as the LORD had spoken to him; and Lot went with him. Now Abram was seventy-five years old when he departed from Haran."*
> (Genesis 12:1-4)

God wants to bless people. But there are cases where God selects someone to bless, and there are cases where a person chooses on his own to enter within the boundaries of God's blessings. Some people choose to enter into God's blessings, but then leave it. And then there are those who have nothing to do with blessings. Let's first look at the cases where God selects someone to bless.

Abraham, the Father of Faith

God is the first and the last, the beginning and the end. He designed the flow of the history of mankind and He continues to lead it as well. Let's say for instance that we're building a house. We come up with a design by estimating how long the construction will take, what kinds of materials will be used, how much steel and how much concrete we will need, and how many pillars we will need. So if we were to look at the history of mankind as God's house, there are several key people who are kind of like the 'pillars' of God's house.

In order to carry out His providence, God chooses certain people to tell others that God is indeed a living God and that Heaven and Hell actually exist. This is why God chooses these people to act as pillars. And we can see they are quite different from ordinary people in terms of the makeup of their hearts and their passion for God. One of these people is Abraham.

He lived about four thousand years ago. He was born in Ur of the Chaldeans. Ur was an ancient Sumerian city located downstream and on the west bank of the Euphrates River in the cradle of the Mesopotamian civilization.

Abraham was so loved and acknowledged by God that he was called "a friend of God". He enjoyed all kinds of blessings from God including offspring, wealth, health, and a long life. Not only that, but as God said in Genesis 18:17, *"Shall I hide from Abraham what I am about to do?"* God clearly revealed to Abraham even the events that were to come in the future.

God considers faith as righteousness and gives His blessings

What do you think God saw in Abraham that pleased Him so much that He poured so many blessings upon him? Genesis 15:6 says, *"Then he believed in the LORD; and He reckoned it to him as righteousness."* God considered Abraham's faith as righteousness.

God said to him, *"Go forth from your country, and from your relatives and from your father's house, to the land which I will show you; and I will make you a great nation, and I will bless you, and make your name great; and so you shall be a blessing"* (Genesis 12:1-2). God didn't tell him exactly where to go, or explain what kind of land he should expect either. God did not give him a detailed plan about how he should live after leaving his hometown. He simply told him to leave.

What if Abraham had had fleshly thoughts? It's obvious that once he left his father's house, he would become a wanderer and a rover. He probably would have been sneered at. If he had considered these things, he might not have been able to obey. However, Abraham never doubted God's promise of blessings. He just believed in Him. Therefore he obeyed unconditionally and left. God knew the kind of vessel that Abraham was, and this is why God promised that a great nation would be formed through him. God also promised that he would become a blessing.

God also promised to Abraham in Genesis 12:3, *"And I will bless those who bless you, and the one who curses you I will curse. And in you all the families of the earth will be blessed."* After this, when God saw how Abraham gave up his right and sacrificed for his nephew Lot, God gave him another word of blessing. Genesis 13:14-16 says, *"Now lift up your eyes and look from the place where you are, northward and southward and eastward and westward; for all the land which you see, I will give it to you and to your descendants forever. I will make your descendants as the dust of the earth."* God also promised him in Genesis 15:14-15, *'"...one who will come forth from your own body, he shall be your heir.' And He took him outside and said, 'Now look toward the heavens, and count the stars, if you are able to count them.' And He said to him, 'So shall your descendants be.'"*

After giving Abraham these dreams and visions, He led Abraham through trials. Why do we need trials? Let's say that a coach or trainer chose an athlete with great potential—enough to represent his country at the Olympics. But this athlete cannot automatically become a gold medalist. The athlete must endure and persevere through countless training sessions and put forth strenuous efforts in order to achieve his dream.

It was the same for Abraham as well. He had to obtain the qualities and characteristics he needed to fulfill God's promise by going through trials. So, even while going through these trials, Abraham only responded with "Amen" and did not compromise with his own thoughts. Also, he did not seek his own benefit, or give into selfishness or hate, resentment, complaints, grief, jealousy, or envy. He simply believed in God's promise of blessings and obeyed with perseverance.

Then God gave him yet another promise. In Genesis 17:4-6, God said to Abraham, *"As for Me, behold, My covenant is with you, and you will be the father of a multitude of nations. No longer shall your name be called Abram, but your name shall be Abraham; for I have made you the father of a multitude of nations. I will make you exceedingly fruitful, and I will make nations of you, and kings will come forth from you."*

God makes quality vessels through trials

Some people pray to God having dreams that stem from their greed. Out of greed, they may ask God for a good job or wealth that does not fit them. If we pray like this out of selfishness, we cannot receive an answer from God (James 4:3).

Therefore we must pray for dreams and visions that come from God. When we have faith in God's Word and obey, the Holy Spirit takes over our hearts and guides us, so we can fulfill our dreams. We can't see even one second into the future. But if we follow the guidance of the Holy Spirit, who knows all that is to come in the future, then we can experience the power of God. When we tear down our fleshly thoughts and submit to Christ, the Holy Spirit takes over and leads us.

If God gives us a dream, we have to keep it safe in our hearts. Just because the dream doesn't come true after a day, a month, or a year of prayer, we should not complain. God, who gives us the dreams and visions, at times leads us through trials in order to make us vessels that are worthy of fulfilling those dreams and visions. When we become people who know how to obey God through these trials, that is when our prayers are answered. But because God's thoughts and man's thoughts are different, we must realize that until we are able to break down our fleshly thoughts and obey with faith, the trials will continue. Therefore, we must remember that trials are given to us so we can receive answers from God, so instead of trying to avoid them, we should receive them with thanksgiving.

God prepares a way out, even during trials

If we are obedient, God causes all things to work together for good. He will always give us a way out of the trials. In Genesis chapter 12, you will see that after entering into the land of Canaan, there was a great famine, so Abraham went down into Egypt.

Because his wife Sarah was so beautiful, Abraham was afraid that someone in Egypt might covet her and kill him in order to have her. In that time period, this was quite possible, so Abraham introduced her as his sister. Technically, Sarah was his half-sister, so this was not a lie. But at this time, Abraham's faith was not fully cultivated to the point where he consulted God about everything. So this was a case where he depended on his fleshly thoughts.

Sarah was so beautiful that the Pharaoh of Egypt had her brought into his palace. Abraham thought telling people that his wife was his sister was the best way in the given situation, but this caused him to lose his wife. Through this incident, Abraham learned a great lesson, and from that moment forth, he learned to entrust everything to God.

As a result, God brought great plagues upon Pharaoh and his household because of Sarah, and Pharaoh immediately returned Sarah to Abraham. Because Abraham depended on his fleshly thoughts, he went through a temporary hardship, but in the end, he was unharmed, and he had great material gain including sheep, cattle, servants, and donkeys. As it is written in Romans 8:28, *"And we know that God causes all things to work together for good to those who love God, to those who are called according to His purpose,"* for people who are obedient to Him, God prepares a way out of trials, and remains with them through the trials. They might be in hardships for a moment, but eventually they will pass them with faith and receive blessings.

Let's say someone gets by from day to day on a daily wage. If he observes the Lord's Day, his family will have to go hungry for a day. In this situation, a person of faith will obey God's command and keep the Lord's Day, even if it means going hungry. Then would that person and his family go hungry? Surely not! Just as God sent down manna to feed the Israelites, God will lovingly feed and clothe the obedient as well.

That's why in Matthew 6:25, Jesus said *"Do not be worried about your life, as to what you will eat or what you will drink; nor for your body, as to what you will put on."* The birds of the air do not sow or reap nor do they put up food in storage. The lilies of the field neither labor nor spin. But God feeds them and clothes them. So wouldn't God take care of His own children who obey Him and seek His will, so they do not face hardship?

God blesses even during trials

When we examine those people who acted according to God's Word and kept themselves on the righteous path, we can see that even in the midst of trials, God causes all things to work for good in the end. Even though the current circumstances before their eyes appear difficult and troublesome, ultimately, the circumstances actually end up becoming a blessing.

When the southern kingdom of Judah was destroyed, Daniel's three friends were taken captive into Babylon. Even though they were threatened with being thrown into the furnace, they did not bow down in idol worship, and they did not compromise with the world one bit. Because they believed in God's power, they believed that even if they were thrown into the furnace, God would be able to save them. And even if they weren't saved, they were determined to stick by their faith and not bow down to any idols. This is the kind of faith they showed. To them, the Law of God was more important than the law of their country.

Hearing about the disobedience of these young men, the king became furious, and raised the temperature of the furnace to seven times more than its original temperature. Daniel's three friends were bound and thrown into the furnace. But because God protected them, not so much as a hair on their head was singed, nor was there any smell of fire on them (Daniel 3:13-27).

Daniel was the same way. Even though there was a decree that said if anyone prayed to any man or any god beside the king, they would be thrown into the lion's den, Daniel only obeyed God's will. He did not commit the sin of ceasing to pray, and following his every day routine, he continued to pray facing toward Jerusalem three times a day. Ultimately, Daniel was thrown into the lion's den, but God sent the angels and closed the mouths of the lions so Daniel was totally unharmed.

How beautiful it is to see someone not compromising with

the world to keep their faith! The righteous live by faith alone. When you please God with faith, He will respond with blessings. Even if you are pushed to what seems to be the brink of life, if you obey and show your faith to the bitter end, God will make for you a way out, and He will always be with you.

Abraham was also blessed in the midst of trials. Not only that, even the people that were with him were blessed because of him. Today, water is very precious in the Near East regions where Israel is located. It was also very precious in Abraham's time as well. But wherever Abraham went not only was water abundant, but because he was so blessed, his nephew Lot also shared in the blessings and had large flocks and herds as well as silver and gold.

Back in those days, having many cattle meant abundant food and great wealth. When his nephew Lot was taken captive, Abraham took 318 of his trained servants to go rescue him. This alone tells us how affluent he was. Because of Abraham, who diligently obeyed God's Word, the land and the region in which he dwelled was blessed and the people who were with him were blessed as well.

Even the kings of the neighboring countries couldn't do anything to Abraham because he was so highly esteemed. Abraham received all the blessings one could receive in this lifetime: fame and fortune, power, health, and children. As it is written in Deuteronomy chapter 28, Abraham was the kind of person who received blessings when he came in and when he went out. Also, as a true child of God, he became the root of blessings, and the father of faith. Furthermore, he came to understand the deep heart of God, so that God could even share His heart with Abraham and call him his 'friend'. What glory and blessings!

Abraham's character of vessel

The reason Abraham was so blessed was because he had a good 'character of vessel'. He was a man who had the kind of love described in 1 Corinthians chapter 13 and he bore the nine fruits of the Holy Spirit as described in Galatians chapter 5.

For example, Abraham acted with goodness and love in all things. He never hated nor did he strike up enmity with other people. He never brought attention to another person's weakness and he served all people. Because he had the fruit of joy, no matter what trials came his way, he never became sad or angry. Because he trusted God completely, he could rejoice at all times. Whatever the situation, he never reacted with his emotions or made biased decisions. He was patient, and always he listened for God's voice.

Abraham was also a merciful person. When he had to part ways with his nephew, Lot, even though he was senior to Lot, he gave Lot the first choice in picking the land he wanted. He said "If you go to the left, I will go to the right. If you go to the right, I will go to the left," and he allowed Lot to choose the better land. Most people would think that the person of higher position or rank should have the better choice. However, Abraham was a man who could yield to others and who served and sacrificed himself for others.

Also, because Abraham had cultivated a heart of spiritual goodness, when Lot was about to face destruction along with the land of Sodom, he interceded on their behalf (Genesis 18:22-32). As a result, he received a promise from God that He would not destroy the city if there were just ten righteous people found there. However, Sodom and Gomorrah did not even have ten righteous people, and were destroyed. But even then, God saved Lot because of Abraham.

As it is written in Genesis 19:29, *"Thus it came about, when God destroyed the cities of the valley, that God remembered Abraham, and sent Lot out of the midst of the overthrow,"* God saved Abraham's loving nephew, Lot, so that Abraham would not be saddened in his heart.

Abraham was faithful to God to the point of sacrificing his only son, Isaac, who he received at the age of one hundred. Whether it was teaching his son, or in his relationships with his servants and neighbors, he was so perfect and faithful to all God's household that he could even be considered flawless. He had never rashly confronted anyone; he was always peaceful and gentle. He served and helped others with such a beautiful heart. And he was so self-controlled that with whatever he did, he never behaved inappropriately, or crossed any lines.

Like this, Abraham completely bore the nine fruits of the Holy Spirit that he did not lack any of the fruits. He also had a good heart. After all, he was such a good vessel. Yet becoming a blessed man like Abraham is not a difficult thing at all. We just have to emulate him. Since the Almighty Creator God is our Father, why wouldn't He answer the prayers and petitions of His children?

This process of becoming like Abraham should not be difficult at all. The only difficult part is if our own thoughts get ahead of us. If we completely trust and depend on God and obey Him, then the God of Abraham will take care of us and lead us to the way of blessings!

The Path of Abraham's Move

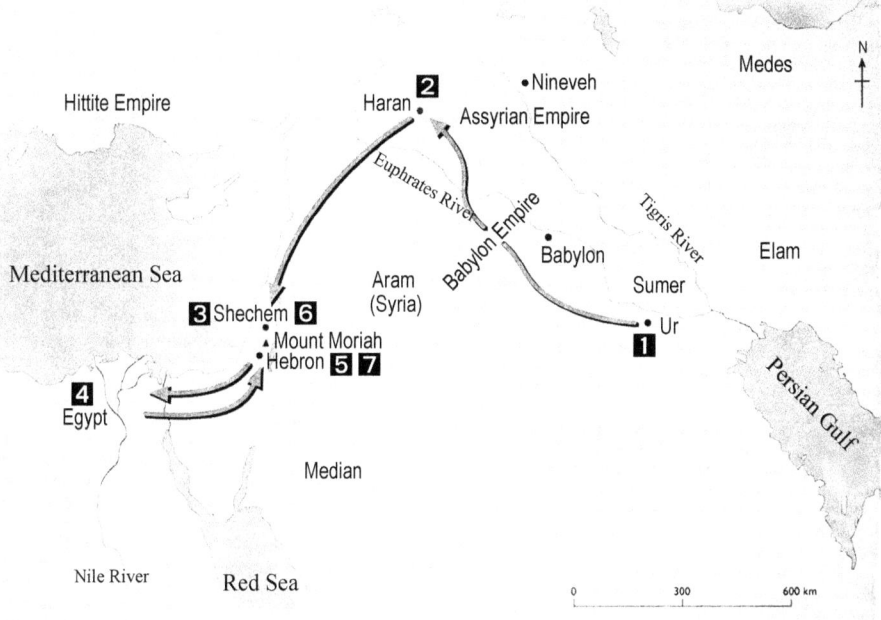

1. Abraham is born in Ur (Genesis 11:27-28)
2. Abraham and his family moves to Haran (Genesis 11:31)
3. Abraham built an altar to the LORD upon arrival in the land of Canaan (Genesis 12:5-7)
4. Abraham went down into Egypt (Genesis 12:10)
5. Abraham built an altar to the LORD by the oaks of Mamre in Hebron (Genesis 13:18)
6. The sacrifice of Isaac in the mountains of Moriah (Genesis 22:1-19)
7. Abraham and Sarah are buried in Hebron (Genesis 23:1-20), 25:7-10)

Glossary and Explanation of Concepts

The obedience and blessings of Noah, a righteous man

"These are the records of the generations of Noah. Noah was a righteous man, blameless in his time; Noah walked with God. Noah became the father of three sons: Shem, Ham, and Japheth" (Genesis 6:9-10).

The first man Adam spent a long, long time in the Garden of Eden. But after he sinned he was banished from the Garden of Eden and later came to live on the Earth. About 1,000 years later, Noah was born as a descendant of Seth, a man who revered God. Noah, who is also a descendant of Enoch, learned from the teachings of his father Lamech and grandfather Methuselah and grew up as a man of truth in the midst of a sinful world. Because he wanted to give God everything he had, he kept his heart pure and did not get married until he discovered that God had a special plan for his life. So at the age of five hundred Noah got married and started a family (Genesis 5:32).

Noah knew about the judgment of the flood and that human cultivation would start all over again through him. Therefore he dedicated his life to obeying God's will. This is why God chose Noah who was a righteous man and who would obey God whole-heartedly in building the ark without giving into his own thoughts, reasons, or excuses.

The spiritual symbolism of Noah's ark

"Make for yourself an ark of gopher wood; you shall make the ark with rooms, and shall cover it inside and out with pitch. This is how you shall make it: the length of the ark three hundred cubits, its breadth fifty cubits, and its height thirty cubits. You shall make a window for the ark, and finish it to a cubit from the top; and set the door of the ark in the side of it; you shall make it with lower, second, and third decks" (Genesis 6:14-16).

Noah's ark was a massive structure: 138 meters long, 23 meters wide, and 14 meters high, and it was built about 4,500 years ago. As a result of the influence of the people of the Garden of Eden, Noah's knowledge and skill was extraordinary, but because he built the ark according to the design God gave him, Noah and his family of eight and all the different types of animals were able to survive during the 40 days of the Flood, staying in the ark for more than a year.

The ark is a spiritual symbolism of God's Word, and going inside the ark symbolizes salvation. And the three decks in the ark signify the fact that the Trinity God—the Father, the Son, and the Holy Spirit—will complete the history of the human cultivation.

Mount Ararat, where the ark landed

The judgment of the flood, which occurred in the midst of God's justice

"Then the LORD said to Noah, 'Enter the ark, you and all your household, for you alone I have seen to be righteous before Me in this time" (Genesis 7:1).

"For after seven more days, I will send rain on the earth forty days and forty nights; and I will blot out from the face of the land every living thing that I have made.' Noah did according to all that the LORD had commanded him" (Genesis 7:4-5).

God gave people many opportunities to repent before the flood. During all the years it took to complete the ark, God had Noah proclaim the message of repentance to the people, but the only people that believed and obeyed Noah was his family. Going into the ark signifies putting all things you enjoyed in the world behind you and casting them away.

Even though the people had gone too far to turn around, God even gave the people a seven days' warning to repent and avoid the judgment. He did not want them to face the judgment. With a heart full of love and mercy, God gave them the chance to the bitter end. However, not a single person repented or walked into the ark. In fact, they sinned even more! Ultimately, they fell into the Judgment of the Flood.

Part 3
Concerning Judgment...

"... and concerning judgment,
because the ruler of this world has been judged."

(John 16:11)

❦

"The LORD judges the peoples; vindicate me, O LORD, according to my righteousness and my integrity that is in me." (Psalm 7:8)

"Yet you said, 'I am innocent; surely His anger is turned away from me.' Behold, I will enter into judgment with you because you say, 'I have not sinned.'" (Jeremiah 2:35)

"But I say to you that everyone who is angry with his brother shall be guilty before the court; and whoever says to his brother, 'You good-for-nothing,' shall be guilty before the supreme court; and whoever says, 'You fool,' shall be guilty enough to go into the fiery hell." (Matthew 5:22)

"... and will come forth; those who did the good deeds to a resurrection of life, those who committed the evil deeds to a resurrection of judgment." (John 5:29)

"And inasmuch as it is appointed for men to die once and after this comes judgment," (Hebrews 9:27)

"For judgment will be merciless to one who has shown no mercy; mercy triumphs over judgment." (James 2:13)

"And I saw the dead, the great and the small, standing before the throne, and books were opened; and another book was opened, which is the book of life; and the dead were judged from the things which were written in the books, according to their deeds." (Revelation 20:12)

Chapter 11

The Sin of Disobeying God

> *"Then to Adam He said, 'Because you have listened to the voice of your wife, and have eaten from the tree about which I commanded you, saying, "You shall not eat from it"; cursed is the ground because of you; in toil you will eat of it all the days of your life. Both thorns and thistles it shall grow for you; and you will eat the plants of the field; by the sweat of your face you will eat bread, till you return to the ground, because from it you were taken; for you are dust, and to dust you shall return.'"*
> (Genesis 3:17-19)

Many people say life is hardship in itself. The Bible expresses that being born into this world and living in it is painful. In Job 5:7, Eliphaz said to Job, who was in turmoil, *"For man is born for trouble, as sparks fly upward."* A person who has little toils to make a living, and a person who has a lot toils for a different problem in life. And after a person works hard for a certain goal, and it seems the goal is reached somewhat, the dusk of life has approached. When the time comes, even the healthiest person experiences death at some point.

No single person can avoid death, so if you look at it, life is like a transient fog, or a lofty cloud. So what is the reason people face all these different kinds of trials in this "rat-wheel" of life? The first and original reason is because of the sin of disobeying God. Through Adam, Saul, and Cain, we can see in detail the outcome of committing the sin of disobeying God.

Adam, the man created in God's image

God the Creator created the first man, Adam, in His own image, and then breathed into his nostrils the breath of life, and he became a living being, or a living spirit (Genesis 2:7). God planted a garden toward the east in Eden and put the man there. Then He said, *"From any tree of the garden you may eat freely; but from the tree of the knowledge of good and evil you shall not eat, for in the day that you eat from it you will surely die"* (Genesis 2:16-17).

And seeing that it is not good for Adam to be alone, God took one of Adam's ribs and made Eve. God blessed them and told them to be fruitful and multiply. He also let him rule over the fish of the sea, the birds of the sky, and over every living thing that moves on the earth (Genesis 1:28). Receiving this great blessing from God, Adam and Eve had plenty to eat, had many descendants, and led a prosperous life.

In the beginning, just like a newborn baby, Adam had nothing registered in his memory. He was completely empty.

However, God walked with Adam and taught him many things so that he could live as the lord over all creation. God taught Adam about Himself, the universe, and spiritual laws. God also taught Adam how to live as a spiritual man. He taught him the knowledge of good and evil. For many years Adam obeyed God's words and lived for a long, long time in the Garden of Eden.

Adam ate the forbidden fruit

It came to pass that one day the enemy devil and Satan, the ruler of the air, instigated a serpent, which is the craftiest of all animals, and tempted Eve through it. The serpent, who was incited by Satan, knew that God had told the man not to eat from the tree at the center of the Garden of Eden. But in order to tempt Eve, the serpent asked, *"Indeed, has God said, 'You shall not eat from any tree of the garden'?"* (Genesis 3:1)

How did Eve answer this question? She said, *"We may eat the fruit of the trees of the garden; but of the fruit of the tree which is in the midst of the garden, God has said, 'You shall not eat it, nor shall you touch it, lest you die'"* (Genesis 3:2-3, NKJV). God specifically said, *"In the day that you eat from it you will surely die"* (Genesis 2:17). Why did Eve change God's word to "lest you die"? "Lest" means "for fear that". These words signify that there is no absoluteness. "Having a fear of dying" and "Surely dying" are different. This proves that she did not inscribe God's words in her heart. Her reply proves that she did not have absolute faith in the fact that they would "surely die".

The crafty serpent did not miss this opportunity and charged right in, *"You surely will not die! For God knows that in the day you eat from it your eyes will be opened, and you will be like God, knowing good and evil"* (Genesis 3:4-5). Not only did the snake lie, it even stoked greed into Eve! And because the serpent blew greed into Eve's mind, the tree of the knowledge of good and evil, which Eve never even thought about touching, or even going near, actually began to look good and tasty. It actually looked good enough to make someone wise! So finally, Eve ate the forbidden fruit, and gave it to her husband to eat as well.

The result of Adam's sin of disobeying God

So this is how Adam, the progenitor of mankind, came to disobey God's command. Because Adam and Eve did not concretely inscribe God's word in their hearts, they fell into the temptation of the enemy devil and Satan and disobeyed God's command. So, just as God had said, Adam and Eve came to 'surely die'.

However, as we read the Bible, we see they did not die right away. They actually lived many more years and had many children. When God said, "You will surely die," He did not just mean a simple physical death where one stops breathing. He was referring to the fundamental death, which is the dying of spirit. Originally, man was created with a spirit that could communicate with God, a soul which was controlled by the spirit, and the body, which served as a tabernacle for the spirit and soul (1 Thessalonians 5:23). So when man broke God's command, the spirit, which is the master of man, died.

And because man's spirit died as a result of the sin of disobeying God, his communication with God was severed, so he could not live in the Garden of Eden anymore. This is because a sinner cannot co-exist with God in His presence. This is when the hardship of mankind began. The woman's pain in childbirth was greatly multiplied, in pain she would bring forth children; her desire would be for her husband, and he would rule over her. And man had to toil all the days of his life to eat of the ground which was cursed because of him (Genesis 3:16-17). All of creation was cursed together with Adam, and had to suffer with him. On top of it all, all the descendants of Adam, born from his bloodline, were born as sinners and were set on the path of death.

The reason God put the tree of the knowledge of good and evil

Some may wonder, "Did the Almighty God not know that Adam was going to eat the forbidden fruit? If He knew, why did He put it in the Garden of Eden and allowed Adam to disobey? If the forbidden fruit didn't exist, wouldn't that have prevented Adam from sinning?" However, If God didn't place the forbidden fruit in the Garden, would Adam and Eve have experienced thanksgiving, joy, happiness, and love? God's purpose for placing the forbidden fruit in the Garden of Eden was not to make us go the way of death. It was the providence of God, to teach us relativity.

Because everything in the Garden of Eden is of the truth, the people in the Garden cannot understand what untruth is. Because evil does not exist there, people do not know what hate, suffering, sickness, or death really is. So relatively speaking, the people there cannot understand what a truly happy life it is that they experience. Since they have never experienced unhappiness, they do not know what true happiness and true unhappiness is. That is why the tree of the knowledge of good and evil was necessary.

God wanted to have true children who understand what true love and happiness are. If the first man Adam knew what true happiness was when he was in the Garden of Eden, then how could he have disobeyed God? This is why God placed the tree of the knowledge in the Garden, and is cultivating man here on earth so man can learn the relativity of things. Through this cultivation process, man experiences both triumph and failure, good and bad, all through relativity. Only when man learns the truth through this process, can he truly understand and love God from the depths of his heart.

The way to be free from the curse caused by sin

While Adam was living in the Garden of Eden, he obeyed God and learned about goodness from God. But after he disobeyed, his descendants became slaves to the enemy devil, and they became more and more tainted by evil as generations passed. The more time passed, the more evil they became. Not only were they born with the sin they inherited from their parents, but they also registered more sin in their mind as they grew and learned through what they saw and heard. God knew Adam was going to eat the forbidden fruit. He knew this whole world would become filled with sin. He also knew man would go the way of death. That is why He prepared the Savior, Jesus

Christ, before the ages. When the appointed time came, He sent Jesus into this world.

In order to teach people God's will, Jesus spread the gospel of the kingdom of heaven and performed signs and wonders. Then He hung on the cross and shed His sacred blood to pay the price of all mankind's sin. Therefore, anyone who accepts Jesus Christ receives the Holy Spirit as a gift. The way to salvation was opened up for those who cast out untruth and live in the truth by following the guidance of the Holy Spirit. If men recover the image of God that they once had lost and if they revere God and keep His statutes, which is the whole duty of men (Ecclesiastes 12:13), then they can enjoy all the blessings that God has prepared for them. They can enjoy not only wealth and health, but also eternal life in eternal blessings.

As explained, when we come into the Light, we can be set free from the snare of sin's curse. How peaceful does our heart become after we repent and confess, cast off our sins and make up our minds to live according to God's Word! When we believe in God's Word and receive prayer, we can see how we become free from sicknesses, hardships, trials and tribulations. God takes joy in His children who accept Jesus Christ and live in righteousness, and He frees them from all curses.

The result of Saul's sin of disobedience toward God

Saul became the first king due to the Israelites' request for a king. He was from the tribe of Benjamin, and there was no other who was as elegant and gentle as he in Israel. And at the time Saul was anointed as the king, he was a very humble man who considered himself less than others. But after becoming the king, little by little, Saul began to disobey God's command. He belittled the position of the high priest and acted foolishly (1 Samuel 13:8-13), finally committing the sin of disobedience.

In 1 Samuel chapter 15, God told Saul to completely destroy the Amalekites, but Saul did not obey. The reason why God told him to destroy the Amalekites is recorded in Exodus chapter 17. While the Israelites were heading into the land of Canaan after coming out of Egypt, the Amalekites warred against the Israelites.

For this reason, God had promised to utterly blot out the memory of Amalek from under heaven (Exodus 17:14), and because God does not waiver, He was planning to fulfill this promise hundreds of years later, in the time of Saul. Through the Prophet Samuel, God commanded, *"Now go and strike Amalek and utterly destroy all that he has, and do not spare him; but put to death both man and woman, child and infant, ox and sheep, camel and donkey"* (v. 3).

However, Saul disobeyed God. He brought back King Agag as prisoner, and he also brought back the best of the sheep, the oxen, the fatlings, the lambs, and all that was good. He wanted to show his gains to the people and receive their praise. Saul did what he thought was right in his mind, but disobeyed God. The prophet Samuel explained in a way that Saul would understand, but Saul still did not repent, but rather made excuses (1 Samuel 15:17-21). Saul said he brought back the choice sheep and cattle so the people could make a sacrifice to God.

What do you think God said about this sin of disobedience? 1 Samuel 15:22-23 says, *"Behold, to obey is better than* sacrifice, and to heed than the fat of rams. For rebellion is as the sin of divination, and insubordination is as iniquity and idolatry."* The sin of disobedience is like the sins of divination and idolatry. Divination is sorcery, which is a grave sin subject to God's judgment, and idolatry is a sin which God considers as an abomination.

Finally, Samuel chastises Saul, *"Because you have rejected the word of the LORD, He has also rejected you from being king"* (1 Samuel 15:23). But Saul still does not genuinely repent. Instead, in order to keep a good image, he asks Samuel to honor him before his people (1 Samuel 15:30). What is more terrifying and sad than being rejected by God? But this does not apply just to Saul. It also applies to us today. If we disobey God's Word, then we cannot avoid the consequences of that sin. This applies to our nations and our families as well.

For example, if a servant disobeys the king and acts according to his own whim, he has to pay for the penalty of his sin. In the family, if a child disobeys his parents and goes amiss, how sad would his parents be? Since disobedience causes such a breakdown of peace, pain and suffering follow. As a result of Saul's disobedience to God, not only did he lose his honor and power; but he was tormented by evil spirits, and finally, he died in the battlefield and met a miserable end.

The result of Cain's sin of disobedience towards God

In Genesis chapter 4, we see Adam's two sons, Cain and Abel. Cain farmed, and Abel raised sheep. Sometime later, Cain made a sacrifice to God with the produce from the ground, and Abel made a sacrifice to God with the firstlings of his flock, and their fat portions. God found favor in Abel and his sacrifice, but He did not find favor in Cain's sacrifice.

When Adam was banished from the Garden of Eden, God told him that he must make a sacrifice using the blood of an animal in order to be forgiven (Hebrews 9:22). Adam specifically taught his sons the method of sacrifice by blood, and Cain and Abel knew very well about what kind of sacrifice God wanted. Abel had a good heart, so he obeyed and did exactly as he was taught, and made a sacrifice the way God wanted it. But Cain, on the other hand, made a sacrifice according to his own thoughts, according to his convenience. This is why God accepted Abel's sacrifice, but not Cain's sacrifice.

The same applies to us today. God is pleased with our worship when we worship Him with all of our heart, mind, and utmost, in spirit and in truth. However, if we worship Him according to our own whim, and if we walk the Christian walk simply for our own benefit, then we have nothing to do with God.

In Genesis 4:7, God says to Cain, *"If you do well, will not your countenance be lifted up? And if you do not do well, sin is crouching at the door; and its desire is for you, but you must master it."* God was trying to enlighten Cain so he would not commit a sin. But Cain could not master sin and ended up killing his brother.

If Cain had a good heart, he would have turned from his ways, and together with his brother, he would have made a sacrifice that was pleasing to God, and there would have been no problem. However, because he was evil, he went against God's will. This gave birth to jealousy and murder, which is works of the flesh, and as a result of judgment, a curse came upon him. Ultimately, God said to Cain, *"Now you are cursed from the ground, which has opened its mouth to receive your brother's blood from your hand. When you cultivate the ground, it will no longer yield its strength to you; you will be a vagrant and a wanderer on the earth,"* and from thence, Cain became a man who was constantly fleeing (Genesis 4:11-12).

So far we learned through the lives of the first man Adam, King Saul, and Cain, how grave a sin it is to disobey God, and what great trials and tribulations follow as a result. When a believer who knows God's Word disobeys, that is to disobey God. If a believer is not receiving the blessing of prosperity in all areas of his life, that means that in some way or another, he is committing this sin against God.

Therefore we must destroy the wall of sin that stands between God and us. God sent Jesus Christ and the Word of truth into this world to give true life to mankind who is living in the midst of suffering due to sin. If we do not live according to this word of truth, the outcome is death.

We need to live in accordance with the Lord's teachings that lead us to salvation, eternal life, answers to prayers, and blessings. We must not commit the sin of disobedience by constantly checking within ourselves for sins, repenting, and obeying the Word so that we can receive complete salvation.

Chapter 12

"I Will Blot Out Man from the Face of the Land"

"Then the LORD saw that the wickedness of man was great on the earth, and that every intent of the thoughts of his heart was only evil continually. The LORD was sorry that He had made man on the earth, and He was grieved in His heart. The LORD said, 'I will blot out man whom I have created from the face of the land, from man to animals to creeping things and to birds of the sky; for I am sorry that I have made them.' But Noah found favor in the eyes of the LORD. These are the records of the generations of Noah. Noah was a righteous man, blameless in his time; Noah walked with God."
(Genesis 6:5-9)

In the Bible we can see how great man's sin was during Noah's time. God was so grieved about creating man that He declared He would blot out man from the face of the land through the Judgment of the Flood. God created man, He walked with him, and poured His abounding love out to him, so why did He have to bring down judgment upon man like this? Let us examine the reasons for God's judgment and how we can avoid God's judgment and instead, receive His blessings.

The difference between an evil person and a good person

As we interact with people, we get certain feeling about them. Sometimes we can sense whether they are evil, or good. For the most part, people who grew up in a good environment and received proper teaching have softer personalities and good hearts. On the contrary, people who grew up in harsh environments, seeing and experiencing many evil things that deviate from the truth, are more likely to have personalities that become twisted and they may tend more to be evildoers. Of course, there are those who end up going an untruthful way although they were raised in a good environment as well as those who overcome their unfavorable environment and end up being successful and good-hearted. But how many people could possibly be raised in a good environment and receive good education, and on top of that expend their efforts to live a good life?

If we want to look at good people for examples, we can consider the Virgin Mary who gave birth to Jesus, and her husband, Joseph. When Joseph found out that Mary had become pregnant although he had not shared bed with her, what did he do? According to the Law of that time, a person who committed adultery had to be stoned to death. However, Joseph did not reveal her publicly. He wanted to break his engagement quietly. What a truly good heart he had!

On the flip side, an example of an evil person would be Absalom. When his half-brother, Amnon, violated his sister, he decided in his heart to take revenge. So when he found the opportune time, Absalom killed Amnon. And he even built up resentment against his father, David regarding this matter. Eventually he headed rebellion against his father. All of this evil resulted in a tragic end to Absalom's life.

That is why Matthew 12:35 says, *"The good man brings out of his good treasure what is good; and the evil man brings out of his evil treasure what is evil."* For many people, as they grow up, regardless of their intentions, evil naturally gets planted in them. A long time ago, though it was not as frequent, there were a number of people who were willing to die for their country and their people. However, in this day and age, it is very hard to find people like these. Even though they are becoming tainted by evil, many people don't even realize what evil is, and they live on thinking that they are right.

Why God's judgment comes

When we look at what is recorded in the Bible or the history of mankind, regardless of what time period, when the sins of mankind had reached the zenith and then gone beyond limits, God's serious judgment came. We can categorize God's judgments into three major categories.

When God's judgment falls on unbelievers, it can fall upon a nation as a whole, or upon an individual. There are also cases where God's judgment can fall upon His own people. When the nation as a whole commits a sin that goes beyond the ethics of humanity, a great tribulation falls upon the entire nation. If an individual commits a sin that deserves judgment, God will destroy him. When God's people commit a wrongdoing, they are disciplined. It's because God loves His people; He allows trials and tribulations to come upon them so that they can learn from their mistakes and turn away from them.

As the Creator, God not only manages all the people in the world, but as the Judge He also allows man to 'reap what he sows'. In the past when people did not know God, if with a good heart they searched for God or tried to live in righteousness, God sometimes revealed Himself to them through dreams and let them know that He is alive.

King Nebuchadnezzar of the Babylonian Empire did not believe in God, but God still revealed to him in a dream the events that were to come in the future. He did not know God, but he was generous enough to pick out the elite from among the captives. He taught them about the Babylonian civilization, and even appointed them to key positions in the empire. He did this because at one corner of his heart, he acknowledged a supreme god. So even if someone does not know God, if he tries to have a right heart, God will find a way to reveal that He is the living God, and He rewards that person according to his deeds.

Generally, when unbelievers do evil, God will not discipline them unless it is something very serious. This is because they don't even know what sin is, and they have nothing to do with Him. They are like illegitimate children in a spiritual sense. They will eventually end up in Hell, and they stand condemned already. Of course, if their sin has reached its limit and they bring great harm to others, and their evil goes out of control with no regard for humanity, even if they don't have anything to do with Him, He will not tolerate them. This is because God is the judge who judges between the good and evil of all mankind.

Acts 12:23 says, *"And immediately an angel of the Lord struck him because he did not give God the glory, and he was eaten by worms and died."* King Herod was an unbeliever who killed James, one of Jesus' twelve disciples. He also imprisoned Peter. But when he became proud as if he were a god, God struck him, and worms ate him, and he died. Even if a person does not know God, if his sin exceeds a certain limit, he will receive such a judgment as this.

What about in the case of believers? When the Israelites worshipped idols, strayed from God, and committed all kinds of evil, God did not just leave them as they were. He scolded them and taught them through a prophet, and if they still didn't listen, He punished them so that they would turn from their ways.

It is as it is written in Hebrews 12:5-6, *"My son, do not regard lightly the discipline of the Lord, nor faint when you are reproved by Him; for those whom the Lord loves He disciplines, and He scourges every son whom He receives."* God intervenes when His loving children err in their actions. He reprimands and disciplines them so that they may repent, turn around, and enjoy a blessed life.

* Because the wickedness of man was great

The reason God's judgment came upon the earth was because the wickedness of mankind was great (Genesis 6:5). So what does the world look like when the wickedness of man is great?

First, there is the case where people, together as a whole nation, pile up evil. People can become one with the representative of their nation, like the president or prime minister, and build up sin together. A prime example would be the infamous Nazi Germany and the Holocaust. The whole country of Germany worked together with Hitler to annihilate the Jews. Their method of carrying out this evil act was extremely cruel.

According to recorded history, approximately 6 million Jews who were residing in Germany, Austria, Poland, Hungary, and Russia were savagely killed by means of brutal labor, torture, starvation, and murder. Some died naked in gas chambers, some were buried alive in holes in the ground, and some died terrible deaths as living subjects of human experimentation. So what was the fate of Hitler and Germany, who led these evil acts? Hitler took his own life, and Germany became a totally defeated nation, with a permanent, historical blemish to the country's name. Ultimately, the country was divided into two, East and West Germany. Those guilty of committing the heinous war crimes had to change their names and flee moving from place to place. If they got caught, they generally received the death sentence.

The people of Noah's time received a judgment as well. Because the people at that time were so full of sin, God made the decision to destroy them (Genesis 6:11-17). Up to the day of the flood, Noah shouted out about the judgment to come, but they did not listen even to the end. In fact, until the moment Noah and his family went into the ark, the people were still eating and drinking, getting married, and indulging themselves in pleasures. According to Noah, even as they saw the rain falling, they did not realize what was happening (Matthew 24:38-39). As a result, all people died in the flood with the exception of Noah and his family (Genesis chapter 7).

There is also the record in Abraham's time in the Bible of how God sent down judgment of fire and brimstone on Sodom and Gomorrah because they were so full of sin (Genesis chapter 19). In addition to these examples, we can see throughout history where God brought down various judgments of famine, earthquakes, and plagues, etc. upon a nation as a whole when it was completely full of sin.

Next is a case of an individual receiving judgment, whether the person believed in God or not, if he piled up evil, he was judged according to what his deeds had earned. A person's life could be shortened as a result of his own evil, or depending on the degree of his sin, he would face a tragic end in his last days. However, just because someone dies early does not mean he or she received a judgment; because there are cases like Paul and Peter, who were killed though they led righteous lives. Their deaths were also righteous deaths, so in Heaven, they shine like the sun. There are some righteous people from the past who, after pointing out a truth to the king, were forced to drink a deadly potion which ended their life. In these cases, their death was not the result of a judgment due to sin, but a righteous death.

Even in the world today, whether it is as a nation or as an individual, the sin of mankind is great. On the most part, people do not believe in God as the one true God, and they are full of their own opinions. They either chase after false gods, idols, or they love other things more than God. Sex before marriage has become commonly accepted and the movement of gays and lesbians for the legalization of their marriages is making continued advancement. Not only that, drugs are rampant, fights, enmities, hate, and corruption are everywhere.

There is a description of the end times in Matthew 24:12-14, *"Because lawlessness is increased, most people's love will grow cold. But the one who endures to the end, he will be saved. This gospel of the kingdom shall be preached in the whole world as a testimony to all the nations, and then the end will come."* This is our world right now.

Just as you can't tell if there is filth on your body when you're standing in the dark, because there's so much sin in the world, people are living in lawlessness and yet they do not know that their actions are lawless. Because their hearts are so full of lawlessness, true love cannot be poured into them. Distrust, unfaithfulness, and all kinds of heartaches are widespread because people's love has grown cold. How can God, who is spotless and without blemish, continue to just observe all this?

If a parent loves his child, and the child is going astray, what would the parent do? The parent will try persuading the child to change, and reprimand the child. But if the child still doesn't listen, the parent will even try administering the strap to bring the child around. But if the child does things that are just humanly unacceptable, the parent may end up disowning the child. This is the same with God the Creator. If man's sin is so great that he is no different from animals, God can't help but bring down judgment upon him.

* Because the thought of the heart is evil

When God brings down judgment, He grieves not only

because the sin in the world is so great, but also because man's thoughts are evil. A person with a hardened heart is full of evil thoughts as well. He is greedy, and is always seeking to benefit himself, and he doesn't stop at anything to gain riches, and he's constantly having evil thoughts. This can be true of a nation as well as an individual. It can even be true of believers too. Even though a person confesses to believe in God, if he stores up God's Words merely as head-knowledge and doesn't put it into action, he is going to continue seeking to benefit only himself, so he can't help but always have evil thoughts.

Why do we worship God and listen to His Word? It is to act according to His will and become the righteous people that God wants us to be. But there are so many people who call out "Lord, Lord," and yet do not live according to His will. No matter how much work they claim to have done for God, because their hearts are evil, they will receive judgment; and they will not enter into Heaven (Matthew 7:21). Not keeping God's commands and statutes are considered sin, and faith without action is dead faith, so such people cannot receive salvation.

If we heard God's Word, we need to cast out evil and act according to it. Then, as our soul prospers, we will prosper in all respects; and we will also receive the blessing of health. So illnesses, trials and tribulations will not come. And even if they happen to come, all things work together for good, and they rather become opportunities for blessings.

When Jesus came to this world, people like the good-hearted shepherds, Prophetess Anna, Simeon, and others recognized baby Jesus. However, the Pharisees and Sadducees who professed to be strictly obedient to the Law and taught the Law did not recognize Jesus. If they were immersed in God's Word, then goodness would have been in their hearts, and they should have been able to recognize Jesus and accepted Him. But without being changed from the center of their hearts, they were ostentatious and only focused on appearing holy on the outside. Therefore their hearts were calloused and they could not understand God's will, and they could not recognize Jesus. So depending on how much goodness and how much evil you have in your heart, the outcomes differ tremendously.

God's Word cannot be explained in simple and clear language by human knowledge alone. Some people say that in order to know the exact meaning of the Bible, one must study Hebrew and Greek and interpret from the original text. Then why is it that the Pharisees, Sadducees, and the High Priests did not understand the Bible clearly—which was recorded in their own Hebrew language—and why did they not recognize Jesus? This is because God's Word is recorded by the inspiration of the Holy Spirit and it can only be clearly understood when one is inspired by the Holy Spirit through prayer. The Bible cannot simply be interpreted through literary means.

Therefore, if we have untruth in our hearts or the lust of the flesh, lust of the eyes, or boastful pride of life, then we cannot discover God's will nor act according to it. People in this day and age are so evil that they refuse to believe in God; and not only that, even if they claim to believe in God, they still act in lawlessness and unrighteousness. In sum they do not act according to God's will. This is how we know that God's judgment is near.

* Because every intent of the heart is always evil

The reason God has to judge is because every intent of man's heart is always evil. When we have evil thoughts, the plans that come from these thoughts are evil, and these thoughts ultimately provoke evil actions. Just think about how much evil planning goes on in today's society.

We see people in key leadership positions of a nation demanding bribes in large sums of money, or creating slush funds, and delving in heated quarrels and fights. Unscrupulous methods of gaining admission into public positions, military scandals, and all kinds of different scandals are prevalent. There are children who premeditate their parents' murder in order to take possession of the family wealth, and there are young people who plan all kinds of evil schemes to earn money to spend on debauchery.

Even young children today make evil plans. In order to get money to go to the arcade, or to buy something they really want, they lie to their parents, or even steal. And, since everyone is so busy trying to please themselves, every intent of the heart and every act can only be evil. When a civilization makes rapid advances materialistically, society quickly becomes drenched in a decadent and pleasure-seeking culture. This is exactly what is happening today, just like in the times of Noah when sin reached its full measure in the world.

To avoid God's judgment

People who love God, and those who are spiritually awake

say that the Lord's return is very near. And as it is recorded in the Bible, the signs of the end times, which the Lord talked about, are starting to emerge very clearly. Even non-believers often say we are in the end-times. Ecclesiastes 12:14 says, *"For God will bring every act to judgment, everything which is hidden, whether it is good or evil."* Therefore we must know that the end is near, and we must struggle against sin to the point of shedding blood, and cast out all forms of evil and become righteous.

Those who accept Jesus Christ and whose names are written in the Book of Life in Heaven will gain eternal life and enjoy eternal blessings. They will be rewarded according to their deeds, so there will be some who are placed in positions as bright as the sun, and those who are placed in positions as bright as the moon, or the stars. On the other hand, after the Great White Throne Judgment those whose thoughts of the heart were evil, and whose every intent was evil and who refused to accept Jesus Christ, nor believed in God, will suffer eternally in Hell.

So if we want to avoid God's judgment, as it is recorded in Romans 12:2, we must not conform to the world which is full of all kinds of corruption and sin. We should renew our hearts and be transformed so that we can decipher what God's good, pleasing, and perfect will is, and act accordingly. As Paul confessed, "I die daily," we must submit to Christ and live according to God's Word. In this way, our soul has to prosper, so that we can always have good thoughts, and act out of goodness. Then, we will prosper in all respects of our lives and we will be in good health, and eventually we will enjoy eternal blessings in Heaven.

Chapter 13

Do Not Go Against His Will

"Now Korah the son of Izhar, the son of Kohath, the son of Levi, with Dathan and Abiram, the sons of Eliab, and On the son of Peleth, sons of Reuben, took action, and they rose up before Moses, together with some of the sons of Israel, two hundred and fifty leaders of the congregation, chosen in the assembly, men of renown. They assembled together against Moses and Aaron, and said to them, "You have gone far enough, for all the congregation are holy, every one of them, and the LORD is in their midst; so why do you exalt yourselves above the assembly of the LORD?"
(Numbers 16:1-3)

"As he finished speaking all these words, the ground that was under them split open; and the earth opened its mouth and swallowed them up, and their households, and all the men who belonged to Korah with their possessions. So they and all that belonged to them went down alive to Sheol; and the earth closed over them, and they perished from the midst of the assembly..."
(Numbers 16:31-35)

If we obey the Word, keep His statutes, and walk in the righteous way, we receive blessings when we come in and when we go out. We receive blessings in all areas of our lives. On the contrary, if we do not obey but stand against God's will, then judgment comes upon us. So we should become a true child of God who loves Him, obeys His will wholeheartedly, and acts according to His statutes.

Judgment comes when we stand against God's will

Once there was a man with righteous indignation. He and some of his comrades brought their wills together and planned for a great revolution to help their country. As the day of revolution came closer, the comrades' wills together grew stronger. But betrayal by one of the comrades' caused the whole plan to save their country to fail completely. How sad and tragic it is when one person's error causes many people's good wills from becoming accomplished?

A poor man and woman got married. For many years, the two of them tightened their belts to save. They eventually bought some land and began to lead comfortable lives. Then suddenly, the husband became addicted to gambling and drinking, and consequently he gambled away all of their hard-earned possessions. Can you imagine how great the wife's heartache must have been?

In relationships among people alone, we can see what tragedies occur when people act contrary to each other's will. So what would happen if a person decided to go against the will of God, the Creator of the universe? When you read the book of

Numbers 16:1-3, there is an incident where Korah, Dathan, and On, together with 250 renowned leaders of the congregation rose up against God's will. Moses was their leader, whom God had chosen for them. Together with Moses, the sons of Israel were supposed to become of one mind to overcome the difficult life in the wilderness and enter into the land of Canaan. But this painful event occurred.

As a result, Korah, Dathan, and On, together with their families, were buried alive when the ground beneath them split open and swallowed them up. The 250 leaders of the congregation were also destroyed by the fire of the LORD. Why did this happen? Standing against a leader that God has chosen is the same as standing against God.

Even in our daily lives, instances of going against God occur frequently. Even though the Holy Spirit urges our hearts we just go against it if His will doesn't fit with our own thoughts and desires. The more we act according to our own thoughts and not His, the more we go against God's will. In time we won't be able to hear the voice of the Holy Spirit. Because we act according to our own will, we run into difficulties and hardships.

People who went against God's will

In Numbers chapter 12, there is a scene where Moses' brother, Aaron, and his sister, Miriam, spoke up against Moses because he had married a Cushite woman. They accused him, saying, *"Has the LORD indeed spoken only through Moses? Has He not spoken through us as well?"* (v. 2) Immediately, God's wrath came upon Aaron and Miriam, and Miriam became leprous.

God then scolded the two of them, saying: *"If there is a prophet among you, I, the LORD, shall make Myself known to him in a vision. I shall speak with him in a dream. Not so, with My servant Moses, he is faithful in all My household; with him I speak mouth to mouth, Even openly, and not in dark sayings, and he beholds the form of the LORD. Why then were you not afraid to speak against My servant, against Moses?"* (vv. 6-8).

Then let's see what it means to go against God's will, by observing some examples from the Bible.

1) The Israelites worshipped idols

During the Exodus, the sons of Israel saw with their own eyes the ten plagues that fell on Egypt and the Red Sea being parted in front of them. They experienced so many different kinds of signs and wonders that they had to know that God is a living God. But what did they do while Moses was up on the mountain fasting for 40 days to receive the Ten Commandments from God? They built a golden calf and worshipped it. God set Israel apart as the chosen people, and He taught them not to worship idols. But they acted against God's will and about three thousand of them died as a result (Exodus chapter 32).

And in 1 Chronicles 5:25-26, it is recorded, *"But they acted treacherously against the God of their fathers and played the harlot after the gods of the peoples of the land, whom God had destroyed before them. So the God of Israel stirred up the spirit of Pul, king of Assyria, even the spirit of Tilgath-pilneser king of Assyria, and he carried them away into exile, namely the Reubenites, the Gadites and the half-tribe of Manasseh, and brought them to Halah, Habor, Hara and to the river of Gozan, to this day."* Because the Israelites played the harlot, worshipping the gods of the land of Canaan, God moved the heart of the king of Assyria to invade Israel and take many of them into captivity. The Israelites' action against God caused this disaster.

The reason the northern kingdom of Israel was destroyed by Assyria and the southern kingdom of Judah was destroyed by Babylon, was also because of idol worship.

In today's terms, it's like worshipping an idol made of gold, silver, bronze, etc. It's the same case with people placing the boiled head of a pig on a table and bowing to the spirits of their deceased ancestors. What a shameful scene it is when humans as the most high of all creation bows down before a dead pig and asks it for blessings!

In Exodus 20:4-5 God gives the commandment saying, *"You shall not make for yourself an idol, or any likeness of what is in heaven above or on the earth beneath or in the water under the earth. You shall not worship them or serve them."*

He also clearly mentioned the curses that would come upon them if they took the commandments lightly and did not abide by it. He also stated the blessings they'd receive if they inscribed the commandments in their hearts and kept it. He said, *"I, the LORD your God, am a jealous God, visiting the iniquity of the fathers on the children, on the third and the fourth generations of those who hate Me, but showing loving kindness to thousands, to those who love Me and keep My commandments."*

That's why when we look around us, we can see that families that have a history of idol worship experience many different kinds of sufferings. One day, a church member that had bowed before an idol experienced a hardship. Her mouth, which had been quite normal before, became twisted and deformed so badly that she could not speak properly. When I asked her what happened, she told me that she had gone to visit her family during the holidays and because she couldn't overcome their pressure to bow before the traditional sacrifice to the ancestors, she gave in and bowed. The next day, her mouth had become twisted to the side. Fortunately, she repented completely before God and received prayer. Her mouth was healed and returned to normal. God led her to the way of salvation by giving her a lesson to realize thoroughly idolatry is a way of destruction.

2) The Pharaoh refused to let the Israelites go

In Exodus chapters 7-12, the sons of Israel, who had been slaves in Egypt, tried to leave Egypt under the leadership of Moses. But the Pharaoh wouldn't let them go, and for this reason great calamity fell upon the Pharaoh and Egypt. God the Creator is the author of the life and death of mankind, therefore no one can go against His will. God's will was for the Exodus of people of Israel. But the Pharaoh, whose heart was hardened, interfered with God's will.

Therefore, God brought down ten plagues upon Egypt. During that time the whole nation began to be torn apart. Finally, the Pharaoh reluctantly let the sons of Israel go, but he had resentment in his heart. So, he recounted and he sent his army to go after them, even into the Red Sea which had been parted. Ultimately, the entire Egyptian army that was in pursuit drowned in the Red Sea. The Pharaoh went against God's will to the bitter end, so judgment came upon him. If God showed him many times that He is the living God, the Pharaoh should have realized that God is the One and only true God. He should have obeyed His will. Even by human standards, letting the Israelites go free was the right thing to do.

For one nation to take another entire race as slaves is just wrong. Moreover, Egypt was able to avoid a great famine thanks to Joseph, the son of Jacob. Despite the fact that 400 years had passed, it was an historical truth that Egypt owed Israel for saving it as a nation. But instead of paying Israel back for the grace they received, Egypt pressed them into servitude as slaves. So how evil was that? The Pharaoh, who had absolute power, was a proud person full of greed. That is why he fought against God to the very end, and received His ultimate judgment.

There are people like this in our society today, and the Bible warns that judgment is waiting for them. Destruction awaits those who refuse to believe in God because of their own knowledge and pride and those who foolishly ask, "Where is God?"

Even if they confess to believe in God, if they disregard God's commands with their own whims and stubbornness, if they have animosity or bitterness with others, or if they are a leader in the church and claim to work hard for God's kingdom, and yet because of their jealousy or greed they upset and irritate those around them, they are no different from the Pharaoh.

Knowing that God's will for us is to live in the Light, if we continue to live in the darkness, then we will experience the same kinds of suffering non-believers experience. This is because God continuously warns people, but they do not listen as they go against God's will heading toward the world.

On the contrary, when one lives righteously, his heart becomes clean, and because his heart begins to emulate God's heart, the enemy devil leaves. No matter what kind of serious illness he might have, no matter what kinds of trials and tribulations he might come across, if he continues to act in righteousness before God, he will become strong and healthy, and all the trials and tribulations will disappear. If a house is dirty, cockroaches, mice, and all kinds of dirty pests appear. But if the house is cleaned and disinfected, the pests cannot live in it anymore, and they naturally disappear. This is the same.

When God cursed the serpent which tempted man, He said that it would 'crawl on its belly, eat dust all the days of its life' (Genesis 3:14). This does not mean the serpent will eat the dirt on the ground. The spiritual meaning of this is God telling the enemy devil—which instigated the serpent—to eat the flesh of man, who was formed from the dust. Spiritually, the "flesh" is something that changes and perishes. It signifies the untruth that is the way to death.

Thus, the enemy devil brings temptations, tribulations, and sufferings to men of flesh who sin in the midst of untruth, and ultimately leads them to the way of death. However, the enemy cannot come near holy people who is without sins and who live according to the Word of God. Therefore, if we live in righteousness, then illnesses, trials, and tribulations naturally flee from us.

In Joshua chapter 2, there is a person who, in contrast to the Pharaoh, was a Gentile but helped to fulfill God's will and received blessings as a result. This person was a woman named Rahab who lived in Jericho at the time of the Exodus. After coming out of Egypt and wandering in the wilderness for 40 years, the Israelites had just crossed the River Jordan. They were encamped and ready to attack Jericho at any given moment.

Rahab was not an Israelite but she had heard about them through the grapevine. It occurred to her that the LORD God, who was in control of the entire universe, was with the people of Israel. She also knew that this God was not the kind of god that would kill recklessly or ruthlessly for no reason. Because Rahab knew the LORD God was the God of justice, she protected the Israelite spies by hiding them. Because Rahab knew God's will and helped fulfill His will, she and her entire family was saved when Jericho was destroyed. We too need to carry out God's will in order to lead a spiritual life where we can receive the solution to various problems and receive the answers to our prayers.

3) Eli the priest and his sons break away from God's order

In 1 Samuel chapter 2, we see that the sons of Eli the Priest were lawless men, touching the food that had been set aside for sacrifice to God, and even laying with the women who served at the doorway of the Tent of Meeting. However, their father, Eli the Priest, simply rebuked them with words, and didn't take any action to put an end to the wrong they were doing. In the end, his sons were killed in the war against the Philistines, and Eli the Priest broke his neck and died when he fell from his chair hearing this news. Eli died this way because of his sin of not teaching his sons properly.

The same goes for us today. If we see people around us who commit adultery in the flesh, or who deviate from God's order, and we just accept them without properly teaching them what is right and wrong, then we are no different from Eli the Priest. Here, we must look at ourselves and see if we are like Eli and his sons in any way.

The same goes for spending for personal use the tithes and thanksgiving offerings that had been set aside for God. When we do not give whole tithes and offerings, it is like stealing from God, therefore a curse will fall upon our family, or nation (Malachi 3:8-9). Also, whatever has been dedicated to be offered to God should not be exchanged for anything else. If you have already decided in your heart to make an offering to God, you must carry it out. And if you want to exchange it with something better, you have to offer both the former and the latter.

Also, it is not right for a cell leader or a treasurer of a cell group in the church to use the collected membership fees as they see fit. Using church funds for a purpose different from the intended, or using money set aside for a specific event for a different purpose, also falls into the category of 'stealing from God'. Moreover, putting your hand on God's treasury is stealing just like Judas Iscariot. If someone steals God's money, he is committing a sin greater than the sins of Eli's sons, and he will not be forgiven. If someone committed this sin because he did not know any better, he needs to confess and repent completely, and, he must never commit this sin again. People become cursed because of these kinds of sins. Tragic incidents, accidents, and illnesses come into their lives, and faith cannot be given to them either.

4) The young lads who mocked Elisha and other similar cases

Elisha was a powerful servant of God who communicated with Him and was guaranteed by Him. But in 2 Kings chapter 2, you come across a scene where a large number of youths came out as a group, following Elisha around and mocking him. They were so evil that they followed him from inside the city all the way out of the city, shouting, *"Go up, you baldhead; go up, you baldhead!"* Finally, Elisha couldn't take it anymore, and he cursed them in the name of the LORD, and two female bears came out from the woods and mauled 42 of them. Since the Bible records that 42 of them died, we can infer that the total number of the kids bothering Elisha were actually much greater.

The curses and blessings that come from a servant guaranteed by God will take place exactly as spoken by them. Especially if you mock, slander, or gossip about a person of God, it is like slandering and mocking God. Therefore it is equivalent to going against God's will.

And what happened to the Jews that nailed Jesus on the cross and shouted for His blood to be upon themselves and their descendants? In 70 A.D., Jerusalem was totally destroyed by Roman General Titus and his army. The number of Jews killed at that time was 1.1 million. After that, the Jews were dispersed throughout the world and received all kinds of humiliation and persecution. Then, once again six million were killed at the hands of the Nazis. As you can see, the result of rebelling and going against God's will brings about tremendous repercussions.

Elisha's servant, Gehazi, was in a similar situation. As a disciple of Elijah, who received the answer by fire, Elisha received two times the inspiration that his teacher had. So just being able to serve a master like Elisha was a great blessing. Gehazi personally witnessed many signs that Elisha performed.

If he obeyed Elisha's words and received his teachings well, he probably would have received great power and blessings as well. Unfortunately, Gehazi was not able to do this.

There was a time when by God's power, Elisha healed an Aramean army general, Naaman, who was suffering from leprosy. Naaman was so moved that he wanted to give Elisha a great gift. However, Elisha clearly turned him down. He did this because not receiving the gift was more glorifying to God.

But not understanding his master's will, and blinded by materialism, Gehazi chased after General Naaman, lied to him, and received his gifts. He brought the gifts back and hid them. Elisha already knew what happened, so he gave Gehazi a chance to repent, but he refuted the accusation and did not repent. As a result, Naaman's leprosy came upon Gehazi. It was not just to act against Elisha's will, but it was to act against God's will.

5) Lying to the Holy Spirit

In Acts chapter 5, there is an incident where a couple, Ananias and Sapphira, lie to Peter. As members of the early church, they decided to sell their property and offer the money to God. But when they actually got hold of the money in their hands, greed took hold of them. So they gave only a portion of the money and lied, saying that was all of the money. The two of them died as a result of this act. This was because they did not just lie to man, but they lied to God and the Holy Spirit. They tested the Lord's Spirit.

We shared just a number of examples, but in addition to these, there are many incidences where people go against God's will. God's Law does not exist to punish us but they are there to help us realize what sins are, to lead us to depend on the power of Jesus Christ to overcome them, and eventually to lead us to receive God's abundant blessings. So let us look back at all of our actions to see if any of them ever went against the will of God, and if any did, we should make a complete turn around and act only according to God's will.

Glossary

Furnace and Straw

A 'furnace' is an enclosed chamber in which heat is produced to heat buildings, destroy refuse, smelt or refine ores, etc. In the Bible, the word 'furnace' is used to signify God's tribulations, judgments, Hell, etc. Daniel's three friends, Shadrach, Meshach, and Abed-nego refused to bow down to the golden image Nebuchadnezzar had set up, so they were thrown into a fiery furnace. However, with God's help, they came out alive and unhurt (Daniel chapter 3).

'Straw' is stalks of threshed grain, used as bedding and food for animals, for thatching, and for weaving or braiding, as into baskets. In the Bible, 'straw' symbolically refers to something very insignificant and worthless.

What is arrogance?

Arrogance is not considering others as better than oneself. It is looking down on other people, and thinking 'I am better than them'. One of the most typical conditions where this kind of pride shows up in a person is when a person thinks he is loved and recognized by the head of an organization or group that the individual belongs to. God sometimes uses the method of paying compliments so that an individual can discover if he has a prideful nature.

One of the most common forms of pride is judging and condemning others. We must especially be careful not to harbor spiritual pride which causes us to judge others with the Word of God, which is strictly supposed to be used as the basis to reflect upon ourselves. Spiritual pride is a very dangerous form of evil because it is not easy to discover; therefore we must take special care not to be spiritually arrogant.

Chapter 14

"Thus Says the LORD of Hosts..."

"'For behold, the day is coming, burning like a furnace; and all the arrogant and every evildoer will be chaff; and the day that is coming will set them ablaze,' says the LORD of hosts, 'so that it will leave them neither root nor branch.' 'But for you who fear My name, the sun of righteousness will rise with healing in its wings; and you will go forth and skip about like calves from the stall. You will tread down the wicked, for they will be ashes under the soles of your feet on the day which I am preparing,' says the LORD of hosts."
(Malachi 4:1-3)

God brings every act to judgment; all that is hidden too, whether it is good or evil (Ecclesiastes 12:14). We can see that this is certain if we look at the history of mankind. A proud person seeks for his own gain. He looks down upon others and piles up evil to possess great wealth. However, destruction awaits him in the end. On the contrary, a humble person who reveres

God may seem foolish or he is facing hardship in the beginning, but he receives great blessings and the respect of all men in the end.

God rejects the proud

Compare the two women in the Bible, Vashti and Esther. Queen Vashti was the queen of King Ahasuerus, the king of the Persian Empire.

One day, King Ahasuerus gave a banquet and asked Queen Vashti to come before him at the banquet. However, Vashti, taking pride in her position and remarkable beauty, refused the King's request. The King, who became very angry, removed the Queen from her position. What was different with the situation of Esther, who rose to the position of queen after Vashti?

Esther, who rose to the position of queen, was originally a Jewish captive who was brought to Babylon during the reign of King Nebuchadnezzar. Esther was not only beautiful, but she was wise and humble. At one time her people experienced a great hardship because of an Amalekite named Haman. Then, Esther spent three days in fasting and prayer, and then with the determination that she would perish if she had to, she purified herself, dressed in her royal robes and stood humbly before the King. Because she acted with such humility before the King and all other people, not only did she receive the King's love and trust, but she was also able to carry out the great task of saving her own people.

Since it is written in James 4:6, *"God is opposed to the proud, but gives grace to the humble,"* we must never become a proud person that is thrown out by God. And as it is written in Malachi 4:1, *"All the arrogant and every evildoer will be chaff,"* depending on whether one uses his or her wisdom, knowledge, and power for good or evil, the outcome will be drastically different. A good example of this would be David and Saul.

When David became king, his first thoughts were on God, and he followed His will. David was blessed by God because he humbly prayed before Him, seeking wisdom to know how to strengthen the nation and bring peace to his people.

Saul, however, became overcome with greed and he worried about losing his place as king, so he wasted much of his time trying to kill David, who was receiving the love of God and the love of his people. Because he was proud, he did not heed to the prophet's reprimands. Ultimately, he was disowned by God, and he died a miserable death in the midst of a battle.

So clearly understanding how the LORD God judges the proud, we should cast out pride completely. If we get rid of pride and become humble, God is pleased with us and abides with us through the answers to our prayers. Proverbs 16:5 says, *"Every one that is proud in heart is an abomination to the LORD: though hand join in hand, he shall not be unpunished"* (KJV). God hates a proud heart so much that anyone who joins hands with a proud man will be punished along with him. Evil people tend to flock together with evil people, and good people tend to flock together with good people. This joining of the hands too, comes from pride.

King Hezekiah's pride

Let's take a closer look at how much God hates pride. Among the kings of Israel, there were many who first began their reign loving God and obeying His will, and then over time became proud, went against God's will, and disobeyed Him. One of these kings is King Hezekiah, the 13th king of the southern kingdom of Judah.

King Hezekiah, who became king after his father, Ahaz, was loved by God because he was honest, like David was. He removed the foreign altars and high places, and tore down the sacred pillars within the nation. He completely purged the nation of all idols that God hates, like the Asherah poles which he had axed down (2 Chronicles 29:3-30:27).

But when the nation began to experience political difficulties due to the mistakes of the previous king who was disorderly and unrighteous, instead of depending on and trusting in God, King Hezekiah struck an alliance with nearby countries like Egypt, the Philistines, Sidon, Moab, and Ammon. Isaiah reprimanded King Hezekiah on several occasions that he was committing a reckless act that went against the will of the LORD.

Being full of pride, King Hezekiah did not listen to Isaiah's warnings. Ultimately, God left Judah alone, and Sennacherib, the king of Assyria, struck Judah and defeated it. So King Sennacherib conquered Judah and took 200,000 people as captives. And when King Sennacherib demanded that King Hezekiah pay up huge reparations, Hezekiah met these demands by stripping the Temple and the palace of its precious ornaments and by emptying the national treasury. The articles of the Temple should not be touched by just anyone. But because Hezekiah gave away these sacred articles at his own discretion and for his own survival, God could not help but turn His face away from him.

When Sennacherib continued to threaten Hezekiah even after receiving the huge reparations, Hezekiah finally realized that there was nothing he could do by his own power, so he went before God and prayed, repenting and crying out to Him. As a result, God had mercy on him, and defeated Assyria. We can experience the same lesson in our families, workplace, business, and in our relationships with neighbors, and our brothers and sisters. A proud person cannot receive love; let alone receive help in times of trouble.

The pride of believers

Demons cannot enter into a person who believes in God because God protects him. However, there are cases where demons enter into people who claim to believe in God. How can this happen? God is opposed to the proud. So if a person becomes proud to the point that God turns His face away from him, demons can enter into him. If a person becomes spiritually proud, Satan can cause demons to possess him, and control him and cause him to commit evil acts.

Even if possession does not happen, if a believer becomes spiritually proud, he can offend the truth and as a result become distressed. Since he does not obey God's Word, God is not with him, and everything does not go well in his life. As it is written in Proverbs 16:18, *"Pride goes before destruction, and a haughty spirit before stumbling,"* pride is not beneficial in any way.

In fact, it only brings pain and suffering. We must know that spiritual pride is an absolute parasite, and must be demolished completely.

So how can believers know if they are proud? A proud person thinks he is right, so he does not take other people's criticisms very well. Not acting according to God's Word is also a form of pride, because this shows that one does not respect God. When David broke God's commandment and sinned, God reprimanded him harshly, saying, *"You have despised Me"* (2 Samuel 12:10). So not praying, not loving, not obeying, and not being able to see the log in one's own eye and pointing out the speck in another's eye are all examples of pride.

Looking down on others while judging and condemning them according to our own standards, boasting about oneself, wanting to show off, are all forms of pride. Jumping at every opportunity to get involved in debates and verbal altercations are also forms of pride. If you are proud, you desire to be served and you want to rise to the top. And, while trying to benefit yourself and make a name for yourself, you begin piling up evil.

You must repent about this type of pride, and become a humble person in order to enjoy a prosperous and joyful life. This is why Jesus said, *"Unless you are converted and become like children, you will not enter the kingdom of heaven"* (Matthew 18:10). If a person becomes proud at heart, and he thinks he is always right, and he constantly tries to defend his self-esteem, and involve his own thoughts, then he cannot accept God's Word exactly the way it is and act accordingly, therefore he may not even receive salvation.

The pride of false prophets

If you look in the Old Testament, you see times when kings asked the prophets about future events, and acted according to their advice. King Ahab was the Seventh king of the northern kingdom of Israel, and at the time of his death, domestically, worship of Baal was prevalent, and in the foreign front, the war of aggression with Aram was in full acceleration. This resulted because Ahab refused to heed to Prophet Micaiah's warnings, and trusted in the words of false prophets instead.

In 1 Kings 22, King Ahab asks King Jehoshaphat of Judah to join him in taking back Ramoth-gilead from the hands of the king of Aram. At that time, King Jehoshaphat, who loved God, suggested that they first consult with a prophet to seek God's will before making any decision. Then, King Ahab called together about three hundred false prophets that were always flattering him, and asked them for counsel. They unanimously prophesied Israel's victory.

However, Micaiah, a true prophet, prophesied that there would be defeat. In the end, Micaiah's prophecy was ignored, and the two kings joined together and went to war with Aram. What was the result? The war ended with no victory on either side. And King Ahab, who became cornered, disguised himself as a soldier to sneak away from the battlefield, but was shot by a random arrow and died from loss of blood. This was the consequence of Ahab heeding the prophecies of false prophets and not listening to the prophecy of Micaiah, a true prophet. False prophets and false teachers will receive God's judgment. They will be thrown into Hell—into the lake of sulfur, which is seven times hotter than the lake of fire (Revelations 21:8).

A true prophet with whom God abides has a right heart before God, and thus, he is capable of making correct prophecy. False prophets, those who only carry a title or position ostentatiously, will speak their minds as if it were prophecies and lead their nation into destruction, or lead their people astray. Whether it be within the institution of a family, a country, or a church, if we listen to the words of a good and true person, we will experience peace as we follow goodness. But, if we follow the path of an evil person, we will come to experience suffering and destruction.

The judgment for people who act with pride and evil

1 Timothy 6:3-5 says, *"If anyone advocates a different doctrine and does not agree with sound words, those of our Lord Jesus Christ, and with the doctrine conforming to godliness, he is conceited and understands nothing; but he has a morbid interest in controversial questions and disputes about words, out of which arise envy, strife, abusive language, evil suspicions, and constant friction between men of depraved mind and deprived of the truth, who suppose that godliness is a means of gain."*

God's Word contains all goodness; therefore no other doctrine is needed. Because God is perfect and good, only His teachings are true. However, conceited people, not knowing the truth, speak about different doctrines making arguments and boast about themselves. If we raise "controversial questions", we are arguing that only we are right. If we have "disputes with words" it means we are raising our voices and arguing with words. If we have "envy", it means we want to bring harm to someone if they receive more love than us. We are causing "strife" if we engage in arguments that bring division among people. If we become conceited like this, our hearts become corrupt, and we commit works of the flesh—which God hates.

So if a proud person does not repent and turn from his ways, God will turn His face away from him, and he will receive judgment. No matter how much he cries out, "Lord, Lord," and confesses to believe in God, if he does not repent and continues to do evil, on the Judgment Day, he will be thrown into the fire of Hell along with all the other chaff.

The blessings of the righteous who fear God

A person who truly believes in God will break down their pride and evil deeds to become a righteous man who fears God. What does it mean to fear the LORD God? Proverbs 8:13 says, *"The fear of the LORD is to hate evil; pride and arrogance and the evil way. And the perverted mouth, I hate."* If we hate evil and cast out all forms of evil, we become the people who act out of righteousness in God's eyes.

To people like these, God sheds His abounding love and bestows upon them salvation, answers to prayers, and blessings. God says, *"But for you who fear My name, the sun of righteousness will rise with healing in its wings; and you will go forth and skip about like calves from the stall. You will tread down the wicked, for they will be ashes under the soles of your feet on the day which I am preparing"* (Malachi 4:2-3).

To those who fear God and keep His commands, as it applies to every person (Ecclesiastes 12:13), God blesses them with riches, honor, and life (Proverbs 22:4). Therefore they receive answers to prayers, healing, and blessings so that they can skip about like calves from the stall and enjoy true joy.

In Exodus 15:26, God says, *"If you will give earnest heed to the voice of the LORD your God, and do what is right in His sight, and give ear to His commandments, and keep all His statutes, I will put none of the diseases on you which I have put on the Egyptians; for I, the LORD, am your healer."* So no matter what kind of illness comes his way, a person who fears God will receive healing and live a healthy life, and ultimately, he will enter into Heaven and enjoy eternal honor and glory.

Therefore we must carefully inspect ourselves. And if we find any forms of pride and evil within us, we should repent and turn from those evil ways. Finally, let us become righteous people who fear God with humility and service.

Chapter 15

Concerning Sin, Righteousness, and Judgment

"But I tell you the truth, it is to your advantage that I go away; for if I do not go away, the Helper will not come to you; but if I go, I will send Him to you. And He, when He comes, will convict the world concerning sin and righteousness and judgment; concerning sin, because they do not believe in Me; and concerning righteousness, because I go to the Father and you no longer see Me; and concerning judgment, because the ruler of this world has been judged."
(John 16:7-11)

If we believe in Jesus Christ and open up our hearts to accept Him as our Savior, God gives us the Holy Spirit as a gift. The Holy Spirit leads us to be born again, and helps us to understand God's Word. He works in many ways, like guiding us to live in the truth, and leading us to complete salvation. Therefore, through the Holy Spirit, we must learn what sin is, and know how to tell the difference between what is right and wrong. We must also learn how to act in righteousness so that we can enter into Heaven and avoid the judgment of Hell.

Concerning sin

Jesus told His disciples about how He would have to die by being nailed to the cross and about the tribulations the disciples would have to face. He also encouraged them by telling them how His resurrection and ascension into Heaven would be followed by the coming of the Holy Spirit, and about all the wonderful things they would gain as a result. Jesus' ascension was a necessary step for the sending of the Holy Spirit, the Helper.

Jesus said that when the Holy Spirit comes, He would convict the world concerning sin, righteousness, and judgment. Then what does it mean that the Holy Spirit *"will convict the world concerning sin"*? As it is written in John 16:9, *"concerning sin, because they do not believe in Me,"* not believing in Jesus Christ is a sin, and this means that people who do not believe in Him will ultimately face judgment. Then why is not believing in Jesus Christ a sin?

The God of love sent down His only begotten Son, Jesus Christ, into this world to open up the way of salvation for mankind who became slaves to sin due to the disobedience of Adam. By dying on the cross, Jesus redeemed mankind from all sins, opened up the door of salvation, and became the one and only Savior. Thus, not believing in this fact, knowing it, is in itself a sin. And a person who does not accept Jesus Christ as his or her Savior cannot receive the forgiveness of sin, so he or she will remain a sinner.

Why He judges concerning sin

We can see that there is a Creator God just by looking at all of creation. Romans 1:20 says, *"For since the creation of the world His invisible attributes, His eternal power and divine nature, have been clearly seen, being understood through what has been made, so that they are without excuse."* This means no one can make the excuse that they did not believe because they did not know God.

Even a small wrist watch cannot just happen to fall together by chance just without a human designer and maker. Then how could the most complex and most intricate universe, have just coincidentally been formed on its own? Just by observing the universe, man can discover God's divine and eternal power.

And in this day and age, God shows Himself by manifesting signs and wonders through those people whom He loves. Many people today have probably experienced at least once being evangelized by someone to believe in God, because He is real. Some people might have even personally witnessed a miracle, or heard about it from a first-hand witness. If, even after seeing and hearing about these signs and wonders, a person does not believe because his heart is calloused, then he will ultimately go the way of death. This is what it means when the Scripture says the Holy Spirit "will convict the world concerning sin."

The reason why people don't accept the gospel is usually because they are living a life of sin while chasing after their own benefits. Thinking that this world is everything, they cannot believe in Heaven and eternal life. In Matthew chapter 3, John the Baptist cries out to the people to repent, for the kingdom of heaven is near. He also says, *"The axe is already laid at the root of the trees; therefore every tree that does not bear good fruit is cut down and thrown into the fire,"* (v. 10) and *"His winnowing fork is in His hand, and He will thoroughly clear His threshing floor; and He will gather His wheat into the barn, but He will burn up the chaff with unquenchable fire"* (v. 12).

A farmer sows, cultivates, and reaps the fruits. He then takes the grain into the barn and discards the chaff. God is the same way. God cultivates the mankind, and He leads to eternal life His true children who live in the truth. If they chase after the world and remain sinners, He has to leave them alone to go the way of destruction. So in order to become the wheat and receive salvation, we must become righteous and follow after Jesus Christ with faith.

Concerning righteousness

Under God's providence, Jesus came into this world and died on the cross in order to solve man's sin problem. However, He was able to overcome death, resurrect, and ascend into Heaven because He had no original sin, no committed sins, and He lived in righteousness. In John 16:10 Jesus said, *"...and concerning righteousness, because I go to the Father and you no longer see Me..."* There is an implicit meaning contained in these words.

Because Jesus had no sin whatsoever, He was able to fulfill His mission for coming into this world—He could not be tied down by death, and He resurrected. He also went before God the Father in order to gain Heaven as the first fruit of the resurrection. This is what He calls "righteousness". So when we accept Jesus Christ, we receive the gift of the Holy Spirit, and we gain the authority to become God's children. Through acceptance of Jesus Christ we go from being children of the devil to being born again as holy children of God.

This is what it means to receive salvation by being called "righteous" through faith. It is not because we did something deserving salvation. We receive salvation only through faith and we pay no price. This is why we should always be thankful to God and live in righteousness. We can recover the image of God when we struggle against sin to the point of shedding blood and cast it out to emulate the heart of our Lord.

Why He judges concerning righteousness

If we do not live in righteousness, even the unbelievers mock us. Faith is complete when it is followed up with action, and faith without action is dead faith (James 2:17). It is that the unbelievers judge and condemn from their own perspective, saying, "You say you go to church, and yet you drink and smoke? How can you go around sinning and call yourself a follower of Christ?!" So if, as a believer, you received the Holy Spirit but do not live a righteous life, thereby receiving judgment, this is what the Scripture calls "judgment concerning righteousness".

In this case God will rebuke and discipline His child through the Holy Spirit, so he will not continue living a life of sin. So, the reason why God allows certain types of trials and hardships to come to some people's families, work places, businesses, or themselves is to push them to live as righteous men and women. Furthermore, because the enemy devil and Satan bring accusations against them, God has to allow the trials according to the spiritual law.

The scribes and Pharisees were confident that they were living in righteousness because they thought they knew the Law very well and strictly kept it. But Jesus tells us that unless our righteousness surpasses that of the scribes and Pharisees, we will not enter into the kingdom of heaven (Matthew 5:20). Just calling, "Lord, Lord," does not necessarily mean we have salvation. In order to take possession of Heaven we have to believe in the Lord from the center of our hearts, cast off our sins, and be in the midst of righteousness.

"Living in righteousness" does not just mean listening to God's Word and keeping it in our heads as mere knowledge. It is to become a righteous person by believing in our hearts and acting according to His Word. Just imagine how it'd be like if Heaven was full of swindlers, robbers, liars, adulterers, jealous people, etc. God is not cultivating mankind to bring the chaff into Heaven! God's purpose is to bring in the wheat—the righteous, into Heaven.

Concerning judgment

John 16:11 says, *"...and concerning judgment, because the ruler of this world has been judged."* Here, the "ruler of this world" refers to the enemy devil and Satan. Jesus came into this world because of the sins of mankind. He completed the work of righteousness and left the final judgment. But we can also say that the final judgment has already been made because only through faith in Jesus Christ can man receive the forgiveness of sins and salvation.

Those who do not believe will ultimately go to Hell, so it is like they already received their judgment. This is why John 3:18-19 says, *"He who believes in Him is not judged; he who does not believe has been judged already, because he has not believed in the name of the only begotten Son of God. This is the judgment, that the Light has come into the world, and men loved the darkness rather than the Light, for their deeds were evil."*

Then what can we do to avoid receiving judgment? God told us to be sober-minded, act with righteousness, and stop sinning (1 Corinthians 15:34). He also told us to abstain from every form of evil (1 Thessalonians 5:22). In order to act in righteousness in God's eyes, we should most definitely get rid of outward sins, but we must also cast off even the least of evil as well.

If we hate evil and we make a commitment to remain in goodness, we can cast out sins. You may ask, "It's so hard to cast out even one sin; how can I cast out all my sins?" Think about it this way. If you try to pull out the roots of a tree one by one, it is extremely hard. But if you pull out the main root, all the other smaller sub roots automatically become uprooted too. Likewise, if you focus on getting rid of the most difficult sin first, through fasting and fervent prayer whenever you can, you can cast out other sinful natures too, together with that one sin.

Inside of a person's heart are the lust of the flesh, the lust of the eyes, and the boastful pride of life. These are among the many forms of evil that came from the enemy devil. Therefore man cannot cast out these sins simply with his own strength. That is why the Holy Spirit helps those who make the effort to become sanctified and pray. Because God is pleased with their effort, He will bestow upon them grace and strength. When these four things—the grace and the strength from God above, our efforts, and the help of the Holy Spirit—work together, then we can most definitely cast off our sins.

In order for this process to happen, we must first cut off the lust of the eyes. If something is untruth, it is most beneficial for us not to see it, hear it, or even be near it. Let's say that a teenager saw something obscene on a video or on television. Then through the lust of the eyes, the heart is triggered, and the fleshly desires within the heart become stimulated. Then this causes the teen to think up evil plans and when these plans turn into action, all kinds of problems can occur. This is why it is so important for all of us to cut off the lust of the eyes.

Matthew 5:48 says, *"Therefore you are to be perfect, as your heavenly Father is perfect."* And, in 1 Peter 1:16 God says, *"You shall be holy, for I am holy."* Some people may ask, "How can a person become perfect and holy like God?" God wants us to be holy and perfect. And yes, we cannot accomplish this with our own strength. But this is why Jesus took upon the cross, and this is why the Holy Spirit, the Helper, helps us. Just because someone claims to have accepted Jesus Christ and calls on Him saying, "Lord, Lord", it does not mean he will go into Heaven. He must cast off his sins and live a life of righteousness in order to avoid judgment and enter into Heaven.

The Holy Spirit convicts the world

Then why did the Holy Spirit come to convict the world concerning sin, righteousness, and judgment? This is because the world is full of evil. Just like when we plan for something, we know there is a beginning and an end. If we look at the various signs in the world today, we can see that the end is near.

God the Creator oversees the history of mankind with a clear plan concerning the beginning and the end. If we look at the flow within the Bible, there is a clear distinction between good and evil, and there is a clear explanation that sin leads to death and that righteousness leads to eternal life. To those who believe in God, God blesses them and abides with them. But those who don't believe in Him ultimately receive judgment and go the way of death. God's judgment from long ago is not idle (2 Peter 2:3).

Like the Great Flood during Noah's time, and the destruction of Sodom and Gomorrah during Abraham's time, when the wickedness of man has reached its limit, God's judgment comes right down. In order for the Israelites to be freed from Egypt, God sent down ten plagues upon Egypt. This was a judgment on the Pharaoh for his arrogance.

And approximately two thousand years ago, when Pompeii became so corrupted with extreme perversion and decadence, God destroyed it with the natural disaster of volcanic eruptions. If you visit Pompeii today, the city that was covered in volcanic ash is preserved exactly the way it looked when it was destroyed, and with a single glance, it is possible to see the corruption of its time.

In the New Testament, too, Jesus once rebuked the hypocritical scribes and Pharisees repeating 'Woe to you' seven times. In order to keep the world from falling into judgment and Hell, the world must be convicted and rebuked.

In Matthew chapter 24, the disciples ask the Lord about the signs of His coming and of the end of the age. Jesus explained to them in detail saying that unprecedented great tribulation would come. God will not open up the door of heaven and pour down water or fire as He did in the past, but He will bring judgment that is consistent with the times.

The book of Revelation prophesies that state-of-the-art weapons will appear, and there would be great destruction from an unimaginably large-scale war. Now when God's plan for human cultivation comes to an end, the Great Judgment will come. And when that day comes, there will be a judgment of whether each one will live eternally in Hell, or eternally in Heaven. So how should we be living right now?

Cast out sin and live a life of righteousness

In order to avoid judgment, we need to cast out our sins and live in righteousness. And what's more important is that each person must plow his heart with the Word of God just as a farmer plows the field. We have to plow the roadside, the rocky soil, and the thorny soil and turn them into the good, fertile soil.

But sometimes we wonder, "Why is it that God leaves non-believers alone, and yet He allows such hardships to come to me, a believer?" It is because, just as a bouquet of flowers without roots looks beautiful on the outside but actually has no life, non-believers already stand judged and will go to Hell, so they do not need to be disciplined.

The reason God disciplines us, is because we are His true children, not illegitimate children. Therefore, we would rather be thankful for His disciplining (Hebrews 12:7-13). As parents discipline their children because they love them and they want to lead them to the right way, even if it means administering the rod, because we are God's children, when necessary, God will allow certain hardships to come upon us in order to lead us to salvation.

Ecclesiastes 12:13-14 says, *"Let us hear the conclusion of the whole matter: Fear God, and keep his commandments: for this is the whole duty of man. For God shall bring every work into judgment, with every secret thing, whether it be good, or whether it be evil"* (KJV). To live righteously means carrying out the whole duty of man in our lives. Since God's Word tells us to pray, we should pray. Because He tells us to keep the Lord's Day holy, we should keep it holy. And when He tells us not to judge, we should not judge. In doing so, when we keep His Word and act accordingly, we receive life and we head toward the way of eternal life.

Therefore, I hope you will inscribe all these massages on your hearts to become the wheat bearing the spiritual love described in 1 Corinthians chapter 13, the nine fruits of the Holy Spirit (Galatians 5:22-23), and the blessings of the Beatitudes (Matthew 5:3-12). I pray in the name of the Lord that in so doing you will not just receive salvation but also become God's children who shine like the sun in the kingdom of heaven.

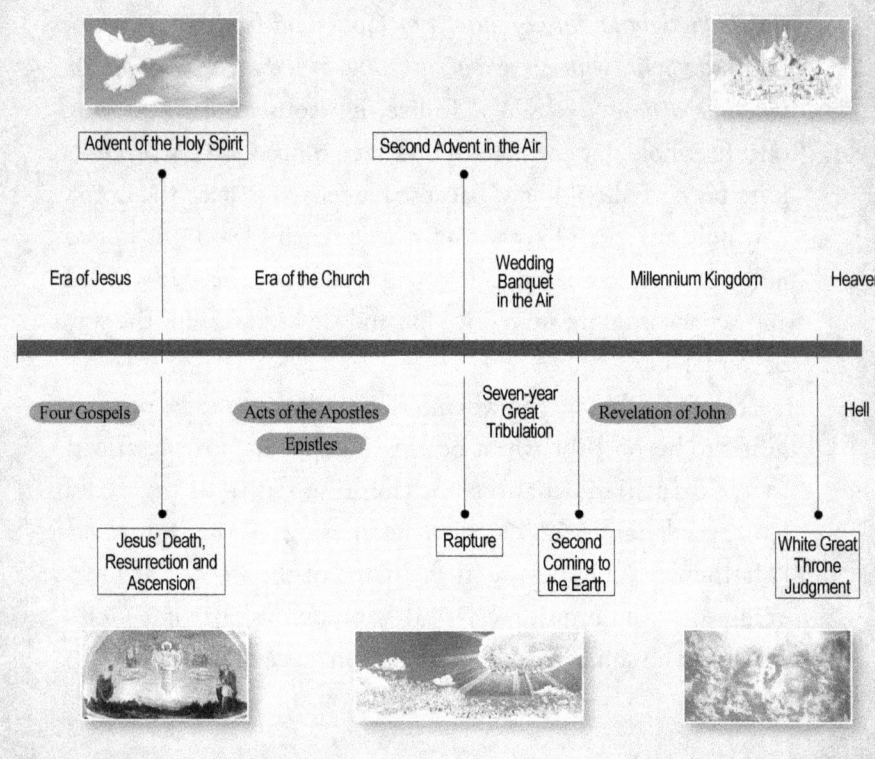

The Author
Dr. Jaerock Lee

Dr. Jaerock Lee was born in Muan, Jeonnam Province, Republic of Korea, in 1943. While in his twenties, Dr. Lee suffered from a variety of incurable diseases for seven years and awaited death with no hope for recovery. However one day in the spring of 1974 he was led to a church by his sister and when he knelt down to pray, the living God immediately healed him of all his diseases.

From the moment he met the living God through that wonderful experience, Dr. Lee has loved God with all his heart and sincerity, and in 1978 he was called to be a servant of God. He prayed fervently with countless fasting prayers so that he could clearly understand the will of God, wholly accomplish it and obey the Word of God. In 1982, he founded Manmin Central Church in Seoul, Korea, and countless works of God, including miraculous healings, signs and wonders, have been taking place at his church ever since.

In 1986, Dr. Lee was ordained as a pastor at the Annual Assembly of Jesus' Sungkyul Church of Korea, and four years later in 1990, his sermons began to be broadcast in Australia, Russia, and the Philippines. Within a short time many more countries were being reached through the Far East Broadcasting Company, the Asia Broadcast Station, and the Washington Christian Radio System.

Three years later, in 1993, Manmin Central Church was selected as one of the "World's Top 50 Churches" by the *Christian World* magazine (US) and he received an Honorary Doctorate of Divinity from Christian Faith College, Florida, USA, and in 1996 he received his Ph. D. in Ministry from Kingsway Theological Seminary, Iowa, USA.

Since 1993, Dr. Lee has been spearheading world evangelization through many overseas crusades in Tanzania, Argentina, L.A., Baltimore City, Hawaii, and New York City of the USA, Uganda, Japan, Pakistan, Kenya, the Philippines, Honduras, India, Russia, Germany, Peru, Democratic Republic of the Congo, Israel and Estonia.

In 2002 he was acknowledged as a "worldwide revivalist" for his powerful ministries in various overseas crusades by major Christian newspapers in

Korea. In particular was his 'New York Crusade 2006' held in Madison Square Garden, the most famous arena in the world. The event was broadcast to 220 nations, and in his 'Israel United Crusade 2009', held at the International Convention Center (ICC) in Jerusalem he boldly proclaimed Jesus Christ is the Messiah and Savior.

His sermons are broadcast to 176 nations via satellites including GCN TV and he was listed as one of the 'Top 10 Most Influential Christian Leaders' of 2009 and 2010 by the popular Russian Christian magazine *In Victory* and news agency *Christian Telegraph* for his powerful TV broadcasting ministry and overseas church-pastoring ministry.

As of December of 2016, Manmin Central Church has a congregation of more than 120,000 members. There are 11,000 branch churches worldwide including 56 domestic branch churches, and more than 102 missionaries have been commissioned to 23 countries, including the United States, Russia, Germany, Canada, Japan, China, France, India, Kenya, and many more so far.

As of the date of this publishing, Dr. Lee has written 105 books, including bestsellers *Tasting Eternal Life before Death, My Life My Faith I & II, The Message of the Cross, The Measure of Faith, Heaven I & II, Hell, Awaken Israel!,* and *The Power of God*. His works have been translated into more than 76 languages.

His Christian columns appear on *The Hankook Ilbo, The JoongAng Daily, The Chosun Ilbo, The Dong-A Ilbo, The Hankyoreh Shinmun, The Seoul Shinmun, The Kyunghyang Shinmun, The Korea Economic Daily, The Korea Herald, The Shisa News,* and *The Christian Press.*

Dr. Lee is currently leader of many missionary organizations and associations. Positions include: Chairman, The United Holiness Church of Jesus Christ; Permanent President, The World Christianity Revival Mission Association; Founder & Board Chairman, Global Christian Network (GCN); Founder & Board Chairman, World Christian Doctors Network (WCDN); and Founder & Board Chairman, Manmin International Seminary (MIS).

Other powerful books by the same author

Heaven I & II

A detailed sketch of the gorgeous living environment the heavenly citizens enjoy and beautiful description of different levels of heavenly kingdoms.

The Message of the Cross

A powerful awakening message for all the people who are spiritually asleep! In this book you will find the reason Jesus is the only Savior and the true love of God.

Hell

An earnest message to all mankind from God, who wishes not even one soul to fall into the depths of Hell! You will discover the never before revealed account of the cruel reality that is in the Lower Grave and Hell.

My Life My Faith II

Dr. Jaerock Lee's autobiography provides the most fragrant spiritual aroma for the readers, through his life extracted from the love of God blossomed in midst of the dark waves, cold yoke and the deepest despair.

The Measure of Faith

What kind of a dwelling place, crown and reward are prepared for you in Heaven? This book provides with wisdom and guidance for you to measure your faith and cultivate the best and most mature faith.

Spirit, Soul, and Body I & II

A guidebook that gives the reader spiritual understanding of spirit, soul, and body, and helps him find what kind of 'self' he has made so that he can gain the power to defeat darkness and become a person of spirit.

Awaken, Israel

Why has God kept His eyes on Israel from the beginning of the world to this day? What kind of His providence has been prepared for Israel in the last days, who await the Messiah?

Seven Churches

The letter to the seven churches of the Lord in the book of Revelation is for all the churches that have existed up until now. It is like a signpost for them and a summary of all the words of God in both Old and New Testaments.

Footsteps of the Lord I & II

An unraveled account of secrets about the beginning of time, the origin of Jesus, and God's providence and love for allowing His only begotten Son Passion and resurrection!

The Power of God

A must-read that serves as an essential guide by which one can possess true faith and experience the wondrous power of God

www.urimbooks.com

www.ingramcontent.com/pod-product-compliance
Lightning Source LLC
LaVergne TN
LVHW012012060526
838201LV00061B/4279